ARCHITECTURE AS THE ETHICS OF CLIMATE

At a time when climate and ethics have become so important to architectural debate, this book proposes an entirely new way for architects to engage with these core issues.

Drawing on Tetsuro Watsuji's (1889-1960) philosophy, the book illuminates climate not as a collection of objective natural phenomena, but as a concrete form of bond in which "who we are"—the subjective human experience—is indivisibly intertwined with the natural phenomena. The book further elucidates the inter-personal nature of climatic experiences, criticizing a view that sees atmospheric effects of climate under the guise of personal experientialism and reinforcing the linkage between climate and ethos as the appropriateness of a setting for human affairs. This ethical premise of climate stretches the horizon of sustainability as pertaining not only to man's solitary relationship with natural phenomena—a predominant trend in contemporary discourse of sustainability—but also to man's relationship with man. Overcoming climatic determinism—regional determinism, too—and expanding the ethics of the inter-personal to the level where the whole and particulars are joined through the dialectics of the mutually-negating opposites, Jin Baek develops a new thesis engaging with the very urgent issues inherent in sustainable architecture.

Crucially, the book explores examples that join climate and the dynamics of the inter-personal, including:

- Japanese vernacular residential architecture
- the white residential architecture of Richard Neutra
- contemporary architectural works and urban artifacts by Tadao Ando and Aldo Rossi

Beautifully illustrated, this book is an important contribution to the discourse which surrounds architecture, climate and ethics and encourages the reader to think more broadly about how to respond to the current challenges facing the profession.

Jin Baek teaches theory and history at the Department of Architecture and Architectural Engineering of Seoul National University. His research focuses on environmental ethics, cross-cultural issues that exist between East Asia and the West in both architecture and urbanism, and the cultural significance of urban regeneration.

"This remarkable study by Jin Baek draws important insights about architectural sustainability and ethics from the non-dualistic philosophy of Tesuro Watsuji (1889-1960). Showing the limitations of current positions that objectify the environment and propose an architecture of personal experimentalism, the book participates significantly in current conversations around the concept of atmosphere and attunement. Drawing particularly from Watsuji's central concept of climate (Jap. *Fudo*) as a trans-subjective and encompassing context for the "social body" involving both culture and nature, Baek demonstrates both the misconception of atmosphere as a subjective effect, and the radical limitations of a discourse on sustainability that treats this problem as a mere technological question reducible to mathematical parameters."

Alberto Pérez-Gómez, Saidye Rosner Bronfman Professor of the
History of Architecture, McGill University, Montreal

"Not since Ruskin's *Ethics of the Dust* (1865) has there been such a persuasive account of the inseparability of architecture's ethical and environmental responsibilities. Baek's study is particularly relevant today, when sustainability discussions suffer from both a narrow dependency on the natural sciences and corresponding neglect of the social and cultural dimensions of resource allocation. Through studies of great architects—Ando, Neutra, Aalto and others—*Architecture as the Ethics of Climate* has reoriented architecture toward more humane, just, and inspiring solutions."

David Leatherbarrow, University of Pennsylvania, USA

"It's rare that architectural writing reaches the depths that Jin Baek's does, rich in scholarship and without undue technicality. Based in the ethico-phenomenological philosophy of Tetsuro Watsuji—one of Japan's most prolific philosophers and a critic of Heidegger's—Baek generates new avenues of architectural thought, ones that give deeper meaning to "sustainability" as well as how architecture might help us live happily among each other."

Michael Benedikt, ACSA Distinguished Professor of
Architecture at the University of Texas at Austin, USA

ARCHITECTURE AS THE ETHICS OF CLIMATE

Jin Baek

Routledge
Taylor & Francis Group

LONDON AND NEW YORK

First published 2016
by Routledge
2 Park Square, Milton Park, Abingdon, Oxon OX14 4RN

and by Routledge
711 Third Avenue, New York, NY 10017

Routledge is an imprint of the Taylor & Francis Group, an informa business

© 2016 Jin Baek

The right of Jin Baek to be identified as author of this work has been asserted by him in accordance with sections 77 and 78 of the Copyright, Designs and Patents Act 1988.

British Library Cataloguing-in-Publication Data
A catalogue record for this book is available from the British Library

Library of Congress Cataloging-in-Publication Data
Names: Baek, Jin, 1969- author.
Title: Architecture as the ethics of climate / Jin Baek.
Description: New York : Routledge, 2016. | Includes bibliographical references and index.
Identifiers: LCCN 2016002705| ISBN 9780415623490 (hb : alk. paper) |
    ISBN 9780415623506 (pb : alk. paper) | ISBN 9781315693941 (ebook)
Subjects: LCSH: Architecture and climate. | Human ecology—Philosophy.
Classification: LCC NA2541 .B34 2016 | DDC 720/.47—dc23
LC record available at http://lccn.loc.gov/2016002705

ISBN: 978-0-415-62349-0 (hbk)
ISBN: 978-0-415-62350-6 (pbk)
ISBN: 978-1-315-69394-1 (ebk)

Typeset in Bembo
by Swales & Willis Ltd, Exeter, Devon, UK

Printed and bound in Great Britain by
TJ International Ltd, Padstow, Cornwall

To my family

CONTENTS

FIGURES

ACKNOWLEDGEMENTS

My interest in Tetsuro Watsuji's *fudo*, or climate, traces back to the period during which I was a doctoral student at the University of Pennsylvania. While working on a work of phenomenology that relates itself to the philosophy of Kitaro Nishida, the father of the Kyoto School, Watsuji's philosophy came fortuitously to my attention. For its potential to offer new insights to the notion of climate and sustainability, my interest in his philosophy and its significance to architecture has deepened during the past several years, and has come to fruition in this work. Recollecting my student days, I would like to express my deep thanks to Joseph Rykwert and David Leatherbarrow who advised my doctoral study and expanded the compass of my interest beyond Nishida, my immediate object of study during the doctoral period. I also thank the recently deceased William LaFleur, then the E. Dale Saunders Professor of Japanese Studies at the University of Pennsylvania for sharing his articles and thoughts regarding Watsuji. I would also like to thank Kazi Ashraf whose teaching included Watsuji's philosophy. Additionally, I thank the recently deceased Dalibor Vesely for the series of extended conversations I had with him, on East Asian thinking including Watsuji's environmental ethics, through meetings in Philadelphia, London, Kyoto and Jerusalem. I thank Kenneth Frampton for the talks he offered at Penn regarding his theoretical perspectives. The talks stimulated my intellectual quest for Watsuji's notion of climate and its interpersonal dimension. I also thank Michael Benedikt who generously shared his works on the ethics of the inter-personal as evident in Martin Buber's thinking. It was fortunate for me to be able to see Alberto Perez-Gomez in Seoul, and enjoy his warm encouragement of my study into Watsuji's phenomenological environmental philosophy. Finally, I thank the teachers I had at Yale including Peggy Deamer and Fred Koetter for their continuous support of my scholarship.

My initial interpretations of Watsuji's philosophy and its implications for architecture have previously been published in several journals: "*Fudo*: An East Asian Notion of Climate and Sustainability" in *Buildings*; "Climate, Sustainability and the Space of Ethics: Tetsuro Watsuji's Cultural Climatology and Residential Architecture" in *The Architectural Theory Review* (http://www.tandfonline.com/); and "The Ecology of 'We' and Ambient Warmth: Richard Neutra's Ecological Architecture" in *Architectural Research Quarterly*. Some parts of "Kitaro Nishida's Philosophy of Emptiness and Its Architectural Significance" published in

Journal of Architectural Education and "*Mujo*, or Ephemerality: the Discourse of the Ruins in Post-War Japanese Architecture" published in *The Architectural Theory Review* (http://www.tandfonline.com/) were reproduced in this work, too. I thank the editors of these journals and the reviewers. In particular, I would like to thank Ute Poerschke, Julio Bermudez, Tom Barrie, Richard Weston, Adam Sharr, Juliet Odgers, Gevork Hartoonian, Anna Rubbo, and Adrian Snodgrass. My researches were presented in various academic and professional meetings including the International Conference on "The Place of Theory in Contemporary Architectural Practice and Education" held at Silpakron University (2013) and International Conference on "Landscape and Imagination: Towards a New Baseline for Education in a Changing World" held at L'École Nationale Supérieure d'Architecture de Paris La Villette (ENSAPLV) (2013). I was also fortunate to be invited to present my researches at the following meetings or schools: PEACE (Phenomenology for East Asian Circle) held at Chinese University of Hong Kong (2014); Graduate seminar at L'École Nationale Superieure d'Architecture of Paris La Villette (2014); Research Center for Intercultural Phenomenology at Ritsumeikan University (2011); Scuola Italiana di Studi sull'Asia Orientale (ISEAS) and École Française d'Extrême-Orient (EFEO) (2010) in Kyoto. I thank those who helped me with the invitation process and those from whom I received warm words of encouragement: Benoit Jacquet, Toru Tani, Takashi Kakuni, Nam-In Lee, Jeff Malpas, Philip Buckley, Jong Kwan Lee, Marc Bourdier, Yann Nussaume, Philippe Nys, Catherine Zaharia, and Tonkao Panin. Tonkao organized a wonderful event in Bangkok that operated as an unforgettable opportunity for me to present my idea about this book project and to see Leatherbarrow, Nadir Lahiji and colleagues from Penn.

My research included field trips to the Richard Young Library and Getty Center in Los Angeles and the study of research archives including Archives-Special Collections at the College of Environmental Design, Cal Poly Pomona, and the Architectural Archives at the University of Pennsylvania. I would like to express my deep thanks to the staff members of these institutions for helping my research activities. My research also included activities in Japan. I cannot express my gratitude enough to Hidetoshi Ohno, Professor Emeritus of the University of Tokyo. My visiting professorship at the Department of Socio-Cultural and Environmental Studies, Graduate School of Frontier Sciences, University of Tokyo operated as an ideal period to research into Watsuji's philosophy and Japanese modern architecture. I also thank Professor Hisao Kohyama, Professor Emeritus at the University of Tokyo, who encouraged my scholarship during the period. Indeed, my debt to Prof. Kohyama goes back to 2001 when I made my first extensive research trip to Japan. I also thank Prof. Kakuni for arranging the details for my visit to *Chochikukyo*, Kouji Fujii's experimental house. I am grateful to Tadao Ando and his staff members, including Yumiko Ando and Chisato Kodaira, for their support of my work in various ways including the supply of drawings and photographs. I also thank Rie Someya and associates of the Office of Arata Isozaki for their generous permission to use their images.

I would also like to take this opportunity to express my thanks to my colleagues of the Department of Architecture and Architectural Engineering, Seoul National University, including those who work in the areas of architectural and urban theories, such as Kwanghyun Kim, Jaepil Choi, Hyuncheol Kim, Bonghee Jeon, and Sohyun Park for formulating an intellectual atmosphere where I could refine my thoughts. I also thank Sunggul Hong and Seung Hoy Kim, the former and current Heads of the Department during the period in which I was working on this book. Sharing ideas and having meals together are the times that enrich my daily life at the campus. I also thank my former colleagues at the University of South Florida and Pennsylvania State University for their continuous collegiality. In particular, Steve Cooke allowed me to reproduce a wonderful photo of his in this book. I thank my graduate and undergraduate students for the times I have had with them to discuss the issues that are dealt with in this book. My laboratory graduate students helped me prepare many drawings in the book and offered editorial support: Hamed Aali, Rohan Haksar, Myongjin Hwang, Seho Kee, Dasoul Park, Yi Liu, Jangkeun Chung, Jihwan Choi and so forth. I also deeply thank Jennifer Schmidt, Fran Ford, Emma Gadsden and Trudy Varcianna of Routledge for their kind and patient guidance in the production of this work.

This work is a testament to the lasting love, support and patience of my family members. Without their understanding, continuous support and encouragement this book would not have been concluded. I share the happiness of completing this work with my wife and children: Youngsun, Soomin and Soochang. I also thank my parents and my mother-in-law for their continuous support of my scholarship. I dedicate this modest book to all who are mentioned in this paragraph.

In continuation of my first book that engaged with interpreting East Asian Christian architecture in reference to the phenomenological tradition of East Asia, this work deals with another aspect of the phenomenological tradition. As with the first book, I confess that this book is open to criticism and I hold myself responsible for any mistakes that may exist in it. Along with introducing and interpreting Watsuji's environmental philosophy, however, this work seeks to transcend conventional comprehension of phenomenology as personal sensationalism and, borrowing Benedikt's words, experientialism and to situate it in reference to the ethics of the inter-personal with implications for sustainable architectural and urban practices. It is my hope that this work succeeds to a degree in this regard.

INTRODUCTION

It is often noted that Frank Lloyd Wright's (1867–1959) organic philosophy idealized the reciprocity between humans and their creations, on one hand, and nature on the other.[1] Strikingly, this idealistic view is witnessed not only in the West but also in East Asia. The definitive example is Daisetz T. Suzuki (1870–1966). Suzuki's emphasis on the humbleness and insignificance of a hut that is merely a four-and-a-half-mat or six-mat room (about ten to fifteen square feet) seems to be effectively contradistinctive with the upscale presence of Wright's Prairie Houses in the leveled mid-western landscape. However, Suzuki was not so different from Wright, when it came to the idealization of the relationship between man and nature. Reminiscent of Wright's organic vision, Suzuki wrote,

> A hut so constructed is an integral part of Nature, and he who sits here is one of its objects like every other. He is in no way different from the birds singing, the insects buzzing, the leaves swaying, the waters murmuring . . . Here is a complete merging of Nature and man and his work.[2]

Indeed, there is a canonic characterization of Japanese traditional architecture: the close relationship between architecture and nature. The small-size Japanese garden with its delicate and exquisite layout of trees, rocks, and a waterfall that forms a pond below is a paradigmatic example (Figures I.1, I.2). A primary architectural device that shapes a close rapport with these features would be *engawa*, a terrace that surrounds the perimeter of a house. This intermediary space of *ma* implies visual openness of the house towards the garden, joining the posture of sitting on the platform and the serenity of the garden.

This harmonized view of nature, however, partially masks the reality of how Japanese nature appears in daily life. It is undeniable that nature in Japan has a different face: unpredictable eruption of disastrous powers such as typhoons and earthquakes, with the Tohoku Earthquake in 2011 being the most recent example. It is in this context that William LaFleur (1936–2010) in his *The Karma of Words: Buddhism and the Literary Arts in Medieval Japan* developed a theory of *mujo*, or ephemerality. *Mujo*, which combines nothing (*mu*) and permanence (*jo*) to create a principle of a cosmological scale, was an idea derived from "the Buddhist teaching that nothing lies outside the law of (*anitya*) or 'necessary change.'"[3] This idea was

FIGURE I.1 Japanese garden 1 (photo by author)

originally meant to suggest impermanence of natural phenomena. It was a category of time based on the ever-changing seasonal cycle of nature. LaFleur claimed that by the end of the twelfth century, however, *mujo* had also begun to suggest instability granted with spatial significance. LaFleur wrote that "it [*mujo*] is no longer limited to the more or less predictable sequence of the seasons; through earthquake, flood, and fire, impermanence/instability takes a totally unpredictable route."[4] *Mujo's* significance extends beyond the somewhat foreseeable cyclical changes in nature in order to embrace nature's unforeseeable and abrupt eruption of disastrous powers, powers that result in a colossal demise of organic and non-organic entities (Figure I.3).

   In contrast with Suzuki's hut nestled in a harmonious relationship with a natural setting, there existed two additional types of huts whose genesis and mode of operation were inseparably joined with Japan's unpredictably disastrous nature, according to LaFleur. The first type adopted a hook-and-eye constructional system to facilitate assembly and disassembly. As verified in Kamo no Chomei's (1153–1216) "Account of My Hut (*Hojo-ki*)," the Buddhist idea of *mujo* came to be expressed through a building being unbound to the land, thus reflecting a medieval hermit's wandering around the Japanese archipelago. That Chinese geomancy was taken over by the portable hook-and-eye constructional system verifies the negation of endurance and rootedness, as if the hut was always ready to float around aimlessly. This type of architecture unfastened, portable and transferrable effectuates a different sense of the ground compared to the Western conception of *terra firma*, or the firm land we unconsciously rely on as the ground of our being. The other type of hut was not transferrable, but stood in a ruinous state to embody *mujo* through its leaky and shaky conditions. For instance, the hut by Saigyo (1118–90) was

FIGURE I.2 Japanese garden 2 (photo by author)

anchored and rooted to the ground, like any ordinary house, compared to the unconventional portability of Chomei's hut. Saigyo's hut was, however, still unique: Unlike any typical dwelling space, Saigyo's hut was "leaky, labile, and coming apart at the seams."[5] While Chomei's is a systematically constructed and completed edifice, carrying out the normal goal of architectural practice, Saigyo's is wrecked, damaged, and devastated. These qualities—the result of nature's weathering and the test of time—would be the focus of immediate repair in a conventional dwelling. However, Saigyo accepted the hut in ruin not only as a legitimate condition, but also as the ultimate destiny in its life. The hut receives the streaks of moonlight and the raindrops through its porous and permeable condition. In this hut, the tears of the poet who meditates upon the ephemerality of life echo with, and intermingle with, the streaks and drops of light and rainwater.

This view of architecture that acknowledges not the beautified imagery of the Japanese nature but its disastrous and transient face of *mujo* extends to the contemporary period. For instance, Arata Isozaki's depiction of the ashes and ruins of mega-structures and of architecture itself embodies the radical ephemerality of *mujo*. For Isozaki, the urban proposals by Metabolism to reflect the metabolic cycle of nature beautify vitality, combined with the metabolic processes of cyclic alteration and vicissitude. Vicissitude notwithstanding, the operational logic of Metabolism was more on the side of maintaining the life of a building by constantly tending the disposable parts, rather than acknowledging the fundamental vicissitude of the building itself. Architecture survives and sustains its life by replacing consumable parts. This optimism of Metabolism espoused vitality, emphasizing life, adolescence, and a purposeful growth. In contrast, Isozaki's ruin was radical as can be seen in his series of photomontages of *Future City* (1962) (Figure I.4) and "Electric Labyrinth" (1968) for the Milan Triennale (Figure I.5). In particular, the latter is more tragic, in that it portrays Japan afflicted not only with natural disasters but also with technological ones. In an article on the 1995 Hanshin-Awaji earthquake, entitled "*Fratture*: On Ruins," Isozaki confirmed the disastrousness of Japanese nature. The earthquake has decomposed all the superficial layers of meaning— all forms of signs such as billboards, neon signboards, and decorations—and has reduced architecture to "sheer materiality,"[6] to dust and eventually to nothing. As with Saigyo, for Isozaki, where the ostentatious utopia is shattered is a ruin that completely decomposes the positivistic materialism. Emerging from a different natural context, Isozaki's imagery of ruins appears more ruinous than the ruins of Western architects such as Le Corbusier (1887–1965), Louis I. Kahn (1901–74) and Aldo Ross (1931–97). The Western discourse of the ruins since the formation of Neo-Classicism have been held as the source of the eternal and enduring power and poetics of architectural form and space before the weathering and perishing power of time (Figure I.6). The ruins function as the inspirational depository of the timeless forms of architecture, rarely associating with evanescence and thereby contrasting with Isozaki's radical ruins.

Returning to the relationship between nature and humans with their artificial construction, it is by now quite clear that Suzuki's characterization of the hut was not necessarily true of the Japanese conception of nature. It is indeed quite striking to note that in his study, Suzuki never mentioned this devastating side of the Japanese nature. Suzuki's bucolic and romantic rhetoric of the close relationship between man and nature, and architecture and nature masks a valid aspect of nature. It does so in two respects. First, as claimed, the rhetoric masks the other face of the Japanese nature, i.e., its calamitous side. Second, Suzuki's rhetoric simultaneously masks how nature *appears* in daily life by anchoring our attention only to the

FIGURE I.3   Tohoku earthquake (© US Navy, source: Wikimedia Commons)

FIGURE I.4 Arata Isozaki, Future City, photomontage, 1962 (courtesy of Arata Isozaki Atelier)

FIGURE I.5 Arata Isozaki, destruction of the Future City, 1968 (courtesy of Arata Isozaki Atelier)

mythical identification of man with nature, an identification in which man becomes "one of [nature's] objects" such as "the birds singing, the insects buzzing, the leaves swaying, the waters murmuring."[7]

The intention of this work is to go beyond the idealized perspective of Suzuki, and to illuminate what the close relationship between man and nature means from a perspective that focuses on how nature *appears* to those who live in daily life. In delving into how nature appears,

FIGURE I.6 Parthenon (photo by author)

the first thing I would like to argue is that one does not experience nature as such, or the meta-physics of nature. This metaphysical attitude doubts the way things appear in our daily life in order to search for essence, or its derivatives such as depth, core or kernel. In place of this aloof attitude, the primary mode that governs the relationship between nature and man is character-ized by a chiasmic bond between what is physically present and, borrowing a philosophical lingo, subjectivity. For example, in the case of a believer of Hinduism, one does not see a light as a neutral scientific electromagnetic radiation of a wavelength but as the undiminished radiance of Shiva (Figure I.7). One may also reflect upon how water appears in the context of the daily life. It becomes instantly clear that one rarely sees water as such, but water as situated such as "a soft lap pool," "a peaceful pond," "a lake on a misty morning," "a sea of turbulence," "a thank-ful shower of rain that brings refreshed coolness on a sweltering summer day," "a rainstorm that shakes the window of my room," "a graciously sinuous river," "a flood that buries down a town completely," and so forth. Examples of how water appears are almost endless, yet no example sees water as a pure element.

The chart on the following page clarifies this point further. This chart presents the different levels in which we engage with water. It also shows how our relationship with water at one level is more primary than our relationship at the level immediately below. Starting from the bottom, before we see H_2O, we see water. Water is closer than H_2O. Before we see water, we see a pool. The pool is closer to us than a physical body of water. Furthermore, before we see a pool, we see a reflecting pool. Before we see a reflecting pool, we see a reflecting pool in a crematorium. Our perception of a part is always transcended by our intuitive understanding of the whole. As we move upward, our relationship with water becomes highly concrete. The behaviors of water such as its stillness at the lowest point in a given topography coalesce with

FIGURE I.7 Believer on the edge of the Ganges (photo by author)

the heart of the human beings in a ceremony in a crematorium. The water resonates with the solemn, peaceful and meditative nature of the ritual, operating as the metaphor of humanity. In contrast, as we move downward, water is dislocated from a concrete human situation to be an element in itself. The metaphysical move that runs contrary to our naïve engagement with water proceeds until one reaches its molecular structure, or dihydrogen monoxide. The daily fabric in which water appears is broken in this abstract attitude.

> 5. A Reflecting Pool in a Crematorium
> 4. A Reflecting Pool
> 3. A Pool
> 2. Water
> 1. H_2O

The emphasis on the appearance of nature in coalescence with humanity is qualitatively different from an anthropocentric appropriation of nature by hegemonic, technical reason that would distort nature into the reservoir of raw materials including other living entities. It is not "a matter of dealing with nature 'as we interpret it' in contrast with nature 'as it really is'"[8] either. Instead, as Erazim Kohak stated, how nature appears points toward a deeper level of experiential union and "a complex of transactional relations" between man and what there is.

Through this pre-reflective and constitutive union, "a meaningful whole *nature*, rather than . . . an aggregate of *what is*" emerges. In fact, as Kohak wrote, "nature as experience is how nature really is."[9] Nature as experience thus corresponds to the spectrum of humanity: from its prone humbleness to upright loftiness, from its desolate loneliness to jovial collective festivity, from its seductive and instinctual Eros to self-transcending Agape, and, finally, from its finitude and temporality to the intuitive awareness of infinity and eternity. One problem of the approach that underscores the non-phenomenological, i.e., metaphysical, truth is that it loosens our relationship with water, which is inseparable. It is this distance that allows us to objectify water as an entity for manipulation, characterizing our attitude toward nature to be hegemonic and instrumental.

There is a Japanese thinker who reflected upon the relationship between man and nature, and the significance of creation half a century before Kohak enunciated environmental ethics. Tetsuro Watsuji (1889–1960), a thinker representative of modern Japan, challenged the manner of comprehending climate in natural science. In *Fudo* (1935), or in its English translation *A Climate: A Philosophical Study* (1965), Watsuji wrote that in respect to the approach in which man and a natural entity are seen as disparate, "we find ourselves examining the relation between object and object, and there is no link with subjective human existence."[10] For him, "the phenomena of climate" should not be seen merely as the phenomena of natural environment but as "expressions of subjective human existence."[11] Climate is not only a set of objective factors, but is intertwined with "who I am" and furthermore "who we are." Climate operates as the mirror of reflection, or the site of self-discovery not only at the individual level, but also at collective level. This is the moment Watsuji's notion of climate entails lessons not merely of subjectivity but also of the inter-personal ethics. It is quite natural that *Fudo* was followed two years later by a work on ethics regarding the relationship between man and man.

Fudo, a Sino-Japanese word, is a combination of two Chinese characters literally meaning "wind and earth." It is "a general term for the natural environment of a given land, its weather, the geological and productive nature of the soil, its topographical and scenic features."[12] As the title of the English translation of *Fudo* indicates, *fudo* could be interpreted as "climate." The translation "climate" remains valid to a degree if understood, by its definition in the *Oxford English Dictionary*: "the characteristic weather conditions of a country or region; the prevalent pattern of weather in a region throughout the year, in respect of variation of temperature, humidity, precipitation, wind, etc., esp. as these affect human, animal, or plant life." However, "climate" seems to fall short in its significance when *fudo* includes other aspects that are related not to weather, but to a larger environmental context such as the topographical and scenic characteristics of a region: its soils, rivers, fields, and pastures in close relationship with the customs and habits of clothing, eating and building. Its limit becomes more obvious when key points in Watsuji's environmental philosophy such as the interwoven dimension between subjectivity and natural phenomena, in conjunction with the inter-personal ethics, are under discussion. Despite these limits, however, this work will occasionally use "climate" as the translation of *fudo*, extending the significance of climate by elucidating its linkage with subjectivity, or "who I am," and its cultural and ethical dimension that arises to the plane of the inter-personal. Following the English convention of plurality, this work will also use *fudos*, a plural form of *fudo*, despite the fact that pluralizing it in the Sino-Japanese language is rarely necessary.

As *fudo* is discussed, "atmosphere," a term that is nearly synonymous with climate in everyday language, comes to one's attention. If one has to differentiate them, climate indicates a stable pattern or character in the midst of the changes in the weather and seasons, and atmosphere varies like the various thermal conditions of a day in a monsoon region. However, their mode of operation is the same, as both climate and atmosphere are predicated upon the combination of the primary elements that are hot, cold, dry, and wet. The discussion of Watsuji's notion of climate offers a new insight into the significance of this atmosphere. In recent architectural discourse, atmosphere is apprehended as impressions or feelings one may get from a setting. Peter Zumthor's comment on atmosphere is a primary example. An atmosphere as an impression or feeling is instantly sensed, rather than deliberated upon for an extended period of time. The source of an atmospheric effect is hard to designate: its nature is holistic and integral, as everything in the setting—"the things themselves, the people, the air, noises, sound, colors, materials, presences, textures, forms, too"[13]—participate in the exudation of an atmosphere. David Leatherbarrow argues that this kind of understanding of atmosphere is limited. It presupposes an atmosphere to be an experience that is personal, i.e., subjective. It also thematizes atmosphere itself, as if it were the main business of architectural creation, as is the case with the idea of "the orchestration of effects."[14] Such position fails to recognize the role of atmosphere in enhancing "the building's capacity to give rise to thought, to embody and communicate ideas."[15] It further fails to see an atmosphere's relation-ship with the setting's practical performance necessarily joined with typical bodily gestures, movements and occupations.[16]

Watsuji's *fudo* does not negate an atmosphere's global and immediate effect, like the atmos-phere of Zumthor. However, Watsuji's thinking clarifies that an atmospheric moment is not a personal, i.e., incommunicable, impression. Rather, an atmosphere is a trans-subjective and encompassing context. It defines those in the context not as being alien to each other but as 'I's who in turn join themselves into 'we' to cope with the atmospheric conditions. The theory of *fudo* thus clarifies the process of the transformation of the 'I' that is embedded in one's encounter with an atmospheric situation and the correlate inter-personal dynamic. Atmosphere exists in this continuum from the natural to the cultural, from the receptive pas-sivity and openness of the sensing corporeality to the creational activity of the bodily subject, and from the individualized sensation to the expansion of the self to form a bigger 'I' in con-junction with others. This is the ultimate thesis of the atmosphere, let alone of climate, in Watsuji's manner of thinking.

Discussing climate is not new in architecture. Indeed, it would be impossible to discuss vernacular architecture without commenting on climate. Along with materials and techniques that are particular to a region, climate is considered a primary factor in defining the distinctive-ness of a region's architecture. Buildings in a hot climate are given deep eaves to create shaded verandas. Sun-breaking devices are also adopted to protect interiors from heat and glare. Cross-ventilation is also essential in removing heat effectively. In contrast, buildings in cold weather regions are constructed out of thick walls with a minimal number of openings. Buildings in a region characterized by long and frequent rainy seasons are often topped with pitched roofs and even stand on stilts to avoid being flooded. Buildings in hot, dry and sandy regions often have wind-catching towers through which hot air is driven out, inviting a wind that cools down the house. A body of water laid along the path of the wind elevates the level of much-needed moisture in the living quarters of the house.

At a theoretical level, climate was an important theme in what is called Critical Regionalism. Kenneth Frampton prescribed being sensitive to "contingencies of climate and the temporarily inflected qualities of local light"[17] as a strategy to confront *placelessness* and the dominance of universal techniques. Frampton saw the loss of aura in the use of artificial light in art galleries, as the mechanical adoption of universal lighting and the resulting placeless, dry evenness renders works of art into commodities. The alternative recommendation was to adopt top-lit, natural light "carefully contrived monitors so that, while the injurious effects of direct sunlight are avoided, the ambient light of the exhibition volume changes under the impact of time, season, humidity, etc."[18] The dialectical play between art and light, and between culture and nature bestows "a place-conscious poetic."[19] Locality also intervenes in the design of the window, the sun breaker being a typical example.

Another aspect Frampton discussed in Critical Regionalism was ventilation. For him, the manner by which ventilation is formed reflects the specificity of local culture. In this regard, air-conditioning was identified as a primary factor leading to universal placelessness. Frampton wrote,

> Here, clearly, the main antagonist of rooted culture is the ubiquitous air-conditioner, applied in all times and in all place, irrespective of the local climatic conditions which have a capacity to express the specific place and the seasonal variations of its climate. Wherever they occur, the fixed window and the remote-controlled air-conditioning system are mutually indicative of domination by universal technique.[20]

Frampton's criticism of air-conditioning is legitimate. It is undeniable that air-conditioning is responsible for the demise of some desired aspects in architectural design. For example, the development of air-conditioning marks a particularly important moment in the history of Florida, because heat was one of the two enemies for the early explorers of the region—the other was the mosquito. While air-conditioning helped transform Florida into an inhabitable land, it also brought some unfortunate side effects. For instance, air-conditioning prompted the end of the impressive residential works of the Sarasota School (a distinctive local school of architecture in Florida).[21] The residential works by the School embodied an active relationship between inside and outside. Here, I do not only mean the visual connection between the two. The works also accommodated the flow of wind from one end of the house to the other through operable doors and windows (Figures I.8, I.9, I.10). Some of the houses also contained gardens inside, as well as in the peripheries (Figure I.11). This kind of planning aims to not only utilize outside gardens as a visual attraction for the interior, but also to conjoin the visual experience with non-visual qualities the gardens emanate. The key element in this organization is the orchestrated flow of wind. Thanks to the flow, different sensorial realities including seeing and smelling reciprocate with, and coalesce into, each other. Like Paul Cézanne (1839–1906), who wanted to paint the smell of a tree,[22] the architects of the Sarasota School sought to realize a sensorial richness in which seeing is smelling and seeing necessarily intermingles with smelling. This sensorial richness restructures the relationship between the interior and exterior, not simply as the matter of visual continuity, or the issue of the nomadic movement of the occupant from inside to outside; the exterior is manifested at the heart of the interior, immediately upon the skin of the occupant.[23]

While Frampton's discussion of climate and his criticism of air-conditioning was foreshadowing the contemporary discourse of sustainability, what is not fully investigated in this relationship of climate and architecture is the sense of climate itself and the ethical basis for sustainable operations such as cross-ventilation. Seeking a design that fits with the local context, climate was presented as a factor to which the architecture of Critical Regionalism must conform. While there is no objection to Critical Regionalism's recommendations such as sensitivity to the range and quality of local light and sensitivity to the daily and seasonal characteristics of wind, rain and humidity, Critical Regionalism did not go further other than stating that climate is an important factor in formulating a place-based architecture. Needless to say, vernacular architecture also rarely inquires into the meaning of climate itself. In the examples listed above, climate is seen as a set of objective forces to which a building has to respond by inventing ingenious devices. This way of understanding climate shows little difference from the scientific conception of the environment indicating natural conditions for the lives of men, animals, and plants on this earth. These conditions are seen as external stimuli and man reacts to them by exercising collective wisdom accumulated through trials and errors.

It is in this context that Watsuji's theory of *fudo* acquires renewed significance. Instead of taking climate as a known factor—an attitude that seems to characterize the contemporary discourse of sustainability—Watsuji's theory leads us to revisit the significance of climate itself. In this process, his environmental philosophy illuminates the inseparable bond between climate and "who I am," or subjectivity, and more importantly highlights the bond between climate and "who we are," or what I would like to call "common subjectivity" in order to offer a theoretical ground for climate to operate as the agency of the inter-personal. A climatic phenomenon is never solitary, as it functions as a field or context in which one and others stand to be imbued by the same forces and characters of the given moment. On account of this collective nature of a climatic experience, any measure of a condition such as a hot summer combined with sizzling humidity is necessarily inter-personal. Climate encourages an orchestration of, and fostering of, the inter-personal. It is also crucial to note that Watsuji's theory of *fudo* as intertwined with "who we are" opens a space for the reflection on the communal as demarcated by a *fudo* and the public as the matter of dealing with the interstitial space between different communities. At this moment one transcends the plane of *fudo* and the communal to arise to the plane of the trans-*fudo* and the public. It is on this plane that one can ruminate upon issues such as the typicality of human praxis beyond regional boundaries. This dimension which I seek to develop from Watsuji's theory of *fudo* is quintessential. Its de-centralizing effect of a region opens a space to overcome conservatism of the regionalist discourse and its essentialist perspective in reference to the issue of cultural identity. What ensues is a

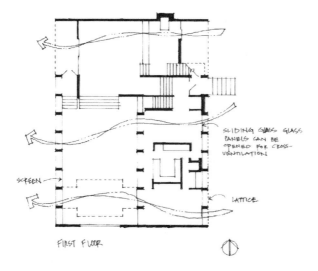

FIGURE I.8 Paul Rudolph, Deering residence, 1958 (image credit: Richard Haas)

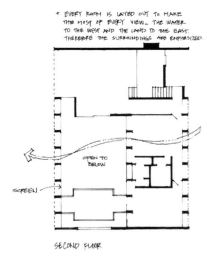

FIGURE I.9 Paul Rudolph, Deering residence, 1958 (image credit: Richard Haas)

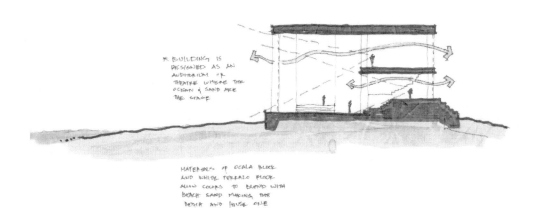

FIGURE I.10 Paul Rudolph, Deering residence, 1958 (image credit: Richard Haas)

dialectical relationship between the demands of the typicality and ideals of the human living beyond regional boundaries, on one hand, and on the other the demands of the local particulars such as climatic idiosyncrasy. In these two-fold demands, the local climatic conditions are not simply an obstacle to overcome in realizing the human cultural intentions, but are instead an agency through and against which the typicality of human praxis is tested and confirmed beyond individual regions.

This work revisits the notion of climate that is bypassed in the contemporary discourse of sustainability by taking Watsuji's theory of *fudo* as the primary reference. It comprises, first, a section that illuminates the meaning and significance of Watsuji's *fudo* and its inter-personal dimension. This section also seeks to theorize the interstitial dimension between one *fudo*

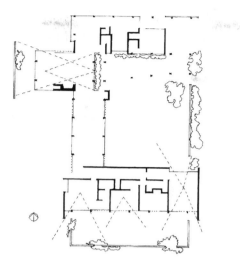

FIGURE I.11   Ralph Twitchell and Paul Rudolph, Denman residence, 1947 (image credit: Richard Haas)

and another as a way of formulating logic to overcome limits of regionalism. The next section deals with an architectural case in reference to *fudo* and its inter-personal ethics: the spatiality of the Japanese vernacular houses. Surprisingly, Watsuji himself made insightful and distinctive comments on the characteristics of the spatial configuration from the perspective of climate and its social dimension. I will contrast Watsuji's reading of the spatiality with that of the Japanese architects during the pre-war period. One immediate objective of this section is to re-examine the taken-for-granted obsession with privacy and to resuscitate the inter-personal as a dimension fundamental to a successful performance of any sustainable measure in the contemporary education and practice of architecture. The following section deals with a modern architect who was deeply influenced by Japanese culture: Richard Neutra (1892–1970). This section reveals Neutra's environmental position as distinctive from other modern architects particularly from the perspective of the sense of climate, and its correlation with human daily activities and its linkage with the inter-personal. In this regard, while there is no evidence that Neutra was specifically aware of Watsuji's *fudo*, this section marks itself as a productive theoretical endeavor to join Neutra's environmental philosophy with Watsuji's in order to clarify and enhance the significance of Neutra's residential and educational works. This section will not only reveal architectural lessons gleaned from Neutra's conception of the environment and the role of an architectural creation, but also correct a view that white modern architecture was altogether unsustainable and environmentally unfriendly. The last chapter discusses contemporary architecture and urbanism with a lens informed by Watsuji's *fudo* and its ethics. It examines both Critical Regionalism in which distinctiveness of climate played a significant role and a criticism of Critical Regionalism from the perspective of the linkage between climate and the inter-personal. The intention is to formulate a *fudo*-based discourse of regionalism and trans-regionalism. When it comes to the domain of the trans-regional, typicality of human praxis and its dialectical relationship with the local particulars including its natural and climatic idiosyncrasy and variableness are the primary interests of this work.

Notes

1   Frank Lloyd Wright, *An American Architecture*, New York: Horizon Press, 1955, p. 190.
2   Daisetz T. Suzuki, *Zen and Japanese Culture*, Princeton, NJ: Princeton University Press, 1993, p. 336.
3   William LaFleur, *The Karma of Words: Buddhism and the Literary Arts in Medieval Japan*, Berkeley: University of California Press, 1983, p. 60.
4   Ibid., p. 61.
5   Ibid., p. 66.
6   Arata Isozaki, "*Fratture*: On Ruins," *Lotus International*, no. 93 (June 1997): 39.
7   Daisetz T. Suzuki, *Zen and Japanese Culture*, p. 336.
8   Erazim Kohak, "Varieties of Ecological Experience," in *Philosophies of Nature: The Human Dimension*, eds Robert S. Cohen, Alfred I. Tauber and Marx W. Wartofsky, Dordrecht; Boston; London: Kluwer Academic Publishers, 1998, p. 258.
9   Ibid.
10 Tetsuro Watsuji, *A Climate: A Philosophical Study*, trans. Geoffrey Bownas, Ministry of Education Printing Bureau, 1961, preface, p. v.
11 Ibid.
12 Ibid., p. 1.
13 Peter Zumthor, *Atmospheres: Architectural Environments – Surrounding Objects*, Bael: Birkhauser, 2006, p. 17.
14 David Leatherbarrow, "Atmospheric Conditions," in *Phenomenologies of the City: Studies in the History and Philosophy of Architecture*, eds Henriette Steiner and Maximilian Sternberg, Surrey, England: Ashgate, 2015, pp. 86–7.
15 Ibid.
16 Ibid.
17 Kenneth Frampton, "Towards a Critical Regionalism: Six Points for an Architecture of resistance," in *The Anti-Aesthetic: Essays on Postmodern Culture*, ed. Hal Foster, New York: New Press, 1983, p. 26.
18 Ibid., p. 27.
19 Ibid.
20 Ibid.
21 Richard Haas, *A Place-Conscious Poetic* (Master of Architecture Thesis, University of South Florida), 2006, p. 6.
22 For the reciprocity between sensorial experiences, see, for instance, Maurice Merleau-Ponty, *The World of Perception*, London and New York: Routledge, 2004, pp. 59–66; *Joachim Gasquet's Cezanne: A Memoir with Conversations*, trans. C. Pemberton, London: Thames and Hudson, 1991, p. 151.
23 This way of designing a garden in conjunction with the flow of wind to bring together the visual and the olfactory, and the visual and the tactile was also commented upon by Richard Neutra. He wrote:

> Yet should hermetical air-conditioning prevail, we know that there will be no such auxiliary as an uncontrolled breeze from the garden. It will no longer help out against the monotony of the interior with an accidental precious whiff of nature's perfume, varied as the seasons unroll, thanks to the blooming lilac bush, the night jasmine, or the pittosporum in the neighbor's garden. Incidentally, it does remain a significant precedent for constructed environment that gardens at least have been sensitively designed on an olfactorial basis too, not only on visual principles.

Richard Neutra, *Survival through Design*, New York: Oxford University Press, 1954, p. 147.

1

TETSURO WATSUJI'S NOTION OF *FUDO* AND ITS CULTURAL SIGNIFICANCE

Positivism fixates our relationship with surrounding things on their instrumental potential as sources of energy preferably with no negative side effects such as pollution. In this context, it is undeniably significant to uncover an environmental philosophy that speaks of what the natural environment is for us beyond the positivistic framing. It is all the more significant if the philosophy operates as a groundwork for the restoration of a broad spectrum of sustainability that takes into consideration the plurality of human living—plurality not in the sense of individualistic and isolated interests of human beings, but in the sense of diverse facets of humanity such as the practical, the ethical and the spiritual. One essential environmental philosophy of this kind is that of Tetsuro Watsuji (1889–1960). His conception of the environment went beyond seeing it as a collection of natural factors—climatic, scenic, and topographical—of a given land. It also overcame the limit of traditional climatology, a field of study that probes into the relationship between the human being and natural phenomena upon the model of force and response, and cause and result, i.e., how climatic features affect the style of living and how the human being in turn overcomes the imposed natural conditions. Distinguishing itself from these approaches, Watsuji's study uncovered a deeper bond between human beings and climatic features. It illuminated how *fudo* operates as the metaphor of subjectivity, or "who we are." *Fudo* is a context in which not only "who I am" but also "who we are" is found and from which the 'I' and others emerge in reciprocity to formulate collective cultural measures in response to climatic phenomena. Watsuji's *fudo* reveals an inseparable link between natural phenomena and the ethics of the inter-personal, opening a path for an extended notion of sustainability that joins the relationship between man and nature with the relationship between man and man—that is, the inter-personal as mediated through climatic phenomena. Watsuji's *fudo* clarifies that without considering the collective *humane* characteristics of a *natural* climatic phenomenon, any sustainable act is inefficient, if not flawed. For this reason, one needs to review and interpret Watsuji's environmental thinking with the aim of elucidating the nature of the relationship between man and the natural environment, and its intrinsic linkage with the inter-personal.

Beyond Heidegger's *Dasein*

Among the thinkers who were influential on Watsuji's philosophy of *fudo*,[1] Martin Heidegger (1889–1976) can be singled out as the most significant figure. Watsuji went to Germany in 1927 to study philosophy under the auspices of the Ministry of Education of the Japanese government. This was the very year Heidegger published *Being and Time*. Heidegger developed his philosophy by criticizing "the Western tradition's over-emphasis on the individual subject separated from its embedded-ness in everyday life."[2] Watsuji adopted the phenomenological embedded-ness of the everyday life from Heidegger. He criticized Heidegger, however, for still being shackled by individualism. In his review of *Being and Time*, Watsuji saw not only the unique contribution of the idea of *Dasein* to humanity but also its lopsided emphasis on the dimension of time and the downplay of spatiality of *Dasein*. *Being and Time* was tainted with what Watsuji saw as the trait of Western individualism that lays stress unjustly on the individual at the risk of disregarding the thrownness (*Geworfenheit*) of the person into a location, or the societal and spatial dimension of the human being. For him, "the limitations of Heidegger's work" is its portrayal of "time not linked with space."[3] *Dasein* was the being of any place, failing to see the fundamental significance of location in the definition of the character of the human being.

Watsuji later qualified further his critique of Heidegger. He acknowledged Heidegger more fully by claiming that the German thinker brought forward the spatiality "constitutive of the being of the subject"[4] in the European intellectual history. Watsuji also praised Heidegger's discussion of "an existential spatiality (*existential Räumlichkeit*) of "a being there (*Dasein*), which is regarded as 'being in the world'."[5] Heidegger's contribution was clear: Uncovering of the pre-presence of the world and the pre-situated nature of the human being before it is abstracted into the subject in confrontation with the object. In this conception of the world and the human being, "space is not inside of the subject nor is the world within space."[6] Spatiality emerges "in its concern with what is at hand,"[7] grounding itself upon man's relationship with tools that are "in their region (*Gegend*) at their place (*Platz*)."[8] Watsuji wrote, "For this reason, the ontological subject is itself spatial, as a being in the world."[9] Heidegger's thinking, however, still left something to be desired. The primacy in Heidegger's spatiality consists of the relationship between the subject and tools joined through care, or *Sorge*, not attending fully to "the relationship of communication among human beings."[10] For Watsuji, the relationship between man and tool is posterior to the relationship between man and man. Watsuji wrote,

> But the concern of *I* with tools is the very ground out of which the relationship between an individual subject versus the objects of nature emerges immediately as soon as its abstraction is carried a step further. The practical relationship between one human being and another is not a major element constitutive of the "concern" he tried to expound. Or rather, it should have been its major element, but this he failed to grasp. This is why spatiality, even though it was conceived of as that structure which is characteristic of the existence of the subject, still stopped short of being a spatiality inherent in the practical interconnections of human beings. This is why he considered temporality to be of far greater importance than spatiality.[11]

What is *fudo*?

Criticizing Heidegger's *Dasein* as an individual being characterized lopsidedly by time at the expense of disregarding spatiality, Watsuji brought to our attention the fundamental significance of spatiality of the human being. Here the spatiality does not mean the significance of space in the scientific sense, but what Watsuji called *fudo*. In Sino-Japanese linguistic tradition, *fudo* literally means wind and earth. However, Watsuji did not treat *fudo* as a natural environment, in which biological, physical and geographical features exert forces on human beings, who in turn transform the environment. Watsuji wrote,

> I wish to treat this natural environment of man not as "nature (*shizen*)" but as "climate (*fudo*) . . . " What I am concerned with is whether the climate we experience in daily life is to be regarded as a natural phenomenon. It is proper that natural science should treat climate as a natural phenomenon, but it is another question whether the phenomena of climate are in essence objects of natural science.[12]

Watsuji's point can be accounted for this way. Temporality conditions our concrete experience of the world. As an abstraction of this concrete experience, we come up with time as a concept. The same goes for our spatial understanding. There are spaces first. Then, space emerges as a concept abstracted from our experiences of spaces. Likewise, before there is nature, there is *fudo*, or climate. Nature as such, or pure nature, is an abstraction. It could be even an illusion that there is such a thing as nature in separation with humanity. *Fudo*, or climate, seeks to overcome this division between man and nature—this dichotomous framework.

For Watsuji, this manner of thinking in which man and nature are treated as two separate entities misses more fundamental bonds between man and the climatic phenomena, bonds suitably connoted in *fudo*. First, *fudo* indicates concrete phenomena in daily life in which, for instance, a physical movement of air is never apprehended as a scientific fact. Rather, the movement appears "as a mountain blast or the cold, dry wind that sweeps through Tokyo at the end of the winter,"[13] or a spring breeze "which blows off cherry blossoms or which caresses the waves."[14] Second, and more importantly according to Watsuji, *fudo* is "the agent by which human life is objectified, and it is here that man comprehends himself; there is self-discovery" in it.[15] It is this reason that "the climatic character is the character of subjective human existence."[16] His examples included "*sabaku*," the Japanese term for desert—one example being the Arabian desert around Aden, which Watsuji himself experienced, and another being the Gobi desert that spans from northern and northwestern China to southern Mongolia. The term "*sabaku*" is a combination of sand (*sa*) and bleakness (*baku*) to signify one single reality. For Watsuji, this coinage indicates the fact that "*sabaku*" is not simply a physical expanse of sand, but a phenomenon of the human heart—aridity, bleakness and loneliness—creating an empathetic unity between man and the sandy landscape.[17] For instance, the terms like *virgin land* or *wilderness* do not indicate nature as it is, but they are already imbued with human values of culture: *virgin* land for its unexplored chastity, and the *wilderness* for its erratic untamable condition. To cite another example, one can think about *warmth*. Warmth is not only a physical quality of a body of air with a certain degree of temperature. It is also a quality that characterizes the relationship between man and man, or the warmth of a person towards others. The same is true of coldness.

In this regard, it is worth introducing Augustin Berque's explication of *fudo*. He apprehended the significance of *fudo* from the perspective of the process of predication (S/P) that transforms *Umgebung*, or the objective physical environment, into *Umwelt*, or the environment filled with semantic meanings of the human world. What makes *Umgebung* a humane world is the transactional relationship between "exteriorization as a projection of human corporeality into the environment"[18] and the symbolic operation that brings the presence of a thing back to our somatic being.[19] The exteriorization and symbolization is a simultaneous process, named by Berque as trajection—that joins projection and retrojection, and cosmization and somatization.[20]

Without this two-way process of trajection, the environment remains alien to human existence. It ends up becoming a pure predicate, absolutizing itself as an independent self-autonomous environment, whether it is called universe, earth or nature. Berque wrote,

> This trajection, by pro/retrojecting our bodyhood-worldhood, is the source of the meaning which things have for us. Things are not objective, since constituting our world, they are fraught with our body; but neither are they mere subjective representations. They are trajective, and this is why they have a meaning. And signs, which are the vectors of this meaning, far from being arbitrary, are embedded in that very pulsation, to and fro, of our existence.[21]

Trajection is the principle that grounds the structural moment of the human being in which the environment is revealed and experienced as *fudo*.

Returning to Watsuji's own account of *fudo*, his point on the pervasive nature of a climatic phenomenon is further significant. Put differently, *fudo* is not something that can be objectified as an entity standing in front of a perceiver. Rather, it formulates a context in which different individuals are located. When one feels cold on a winter's day, for Watsuji, coldness is not at the outside of the perceiver—it is already unfolding at the depth of him or her. From a diametrically opposite angle, this means that the 'I' who is feeling cold is already out in the middle of coldness. A thought that "I feel cold" in which the 'I' and the coldness are treated as two separate objective entities emerges only as an abstraction of this concrete experience in which the 'I,' a being of '*ex-sistere*,' has already transcended its supposed boundary. The 'I' is not lost in this process of acknowledging the trans-individual background of the coldness. Rather, the shared coldness is precisely the ground for the articulation of a distinctive experience of coldness based on one's memory, character and capacity. It is in this context that, in Japan a morning greeting is often characterized by the description of the weather itself: "It is cold this morning" is equivalent to the Western manner of greeting, for example, "good morning." For Watsuji, climate is the basis for the formation of "a 'mutual relation' that discovers ourselves in the cold."[22] The same coldness embraces one person and another, and is articulated distinctively in their hearts. This pervasive nature of a climatic phenomenon indicates that the character of the human subjectivity that corresponds to a climatic phenomenon is also collective. What we call ethos is none other than this shared character of a group of people represented by customs, norms, habits and styles in music, dancing, painting, architecture, theatre and so forth. Watsuji's theory of climate thus establishes a platform for environmental ethics concerned with the bond between climate and collective cultural expressions.

According to Watsuji, what distinguishes the climate of Japan from other parts of the world such as Europe is the coupling of "the seasonal and the sudden."[23] Amidst the cyclic anticipation of the seasons, the Japanese climate manifests variegated articulations from the winter chills to the rainy summer and from the misty morning to the evening shower via the clarity of the atmosphere during the day. In Europe, despite the fact that its "meager humidity content may give rise to . . . fog or mists, it is still not sufficiently rich in change to impress our feelings with any delicacy of light and shade variation. Dull and cloudy days succeed each other in Northern Europe. Clear and fine days are the rule in the South."[24] "This monotony, this absence of variation" in climate is "the mark of Europe."[25] In contrast, in Japan, "the hot season is also the rainy period."[26] The amount of rain in this season is "from three or four times up to six or seven times that of Europe and atmospheric humidity."[27] Humidity and the sun combined give rise to "a marked difference in the tone of the atmosphere."[28] Even a single day of summer is characterized by "refreshing cool" and "a sudden change on the style of the complete clearing of the weather that follows a sharp summer evening shower in Japan."[29] Varieties of thermal conditions are apparent as well: "the cool of a summer's evening, for example, the freshness of the morning, the violent change, sufficient to bring cold at sunset of an autumn day, the morning cold in winter, enough to shrivel the skin, and, after it, the balmy warmth of an Indian summer day."[30] The wide spectrum of the Japanese climate is further verified by the scene of "the bamboo, a native of the tropics, covered in snow,"[31] combining a woody plant of "a tropical belt" with ice crystals of "a frigid zone"[32] (Figure 1.1).

These characteristics of the climate in Japan are not mere environmental facts; these characteristics are "transferred to the description of men's minds and hearts."[33] Climatic characteristics come to be intertwined with "features of man's life."[34] In order to concretize this argument, Watsuji again discusses a European case. "The bright and shadeless clarity and the aridity of Greece's 'eternal noon' presently turned into a type of thinking in which man revealed his all."[35] Watsuji continued:

> Nature's docility—the warm, humidity-free atmosphere, the tender pastures, the smooth limestone—presently turned into the Greek style of clothing, with its sense of freedom . . . its carefree scorn of the need for protection against nature . . . [and] the love of the statue of the naked body.[36]

In contrast, the dualistic climate in Japan exemplifies and cultivates a different ethos, which is "neither the constant fullness of feeling of the tropics nor again the single-toned tenacity of emotion of the cold zone."[37] The cyclical nature of the climate fosters perseverance of, for instance, coldness in expectation of the warmth of spring and the heat of summer. The climate further nurtures the Japanese with "a copious outflow of emotion, constantly changing,

FIGURE 1.1 Bamboos covered in snow 1 (photo by Dongwook Ma, courtesy of the photographer)

yet conceals perseverance beneath this change."[38] In this context, the Japanese sensitivity to "minute and delicate switches of mood"[39] combined with meditative calmness, comes into being.[40]

In this way, Watsuji succeeded in laying a foundation for "minute and delicate switches of mood" for Japanese culture. This moment is particularly important, as one motivation for Watsuji to write *Fudo* was to refute the orientalist claim made by Wilhelm Dilthey (1833–1911). Watsuji criticized Dilthey's *The Imaginative Power of the Poet: Building Blocks for a Theory of Poetry* (*Die Einbildungskraft des Dichters: Bausteine für eine Poetik*) (1887), in which Dilthey defined oriental art as primitively vital and semi-barbarous. For Watsuji, this characterization was groundless. He argued that in the first place "the oriental" was a deeply ambiguous term because of the extensive and fluctuating geological boundaries from the Middle East to the Far East that include multifarious peoples and cultures. In addition, if primitive vitality and semi-barbarity were the characteristics of the Orient, for Watsuji, Europe's supposedly advanced machine civilization was hardly exempt from the same accusations: squeaking cars, honking trams, glaring neon signs, and cranking phones were more primitive and crude. Most importantly, Watsuji thought that the European discourse on the nature of the oriental art, of which Dilthey's definition is an example, failed to understand its real character, particularly that of his own country. By discussing the climate of Japan compared to other parts of the world—particularly Europe—and by seeing it not as an objective environment but as the context of "who we are," Watsuji demonstrates the subtleness and refinement of Japanese culture, and thus proves the erroneousness of Dilthey's characterization.[41]

'*Ex-sistere*' and reflection

One aspect to be noted is the fact that Watsuji's study of *fudo* in different regions in the world, including his own country, came from his extensive exposure to the climates in the world. Indeed, his classification of the climates of the world into three parts—monsoon, desert and meadow—corresponds to the itinerary that he followed in order to study philosophy under the governmental auspices of the Ministry of Education. He left the port of Kobe on March 17, 1927. The ship traveled through the South China Sea, the Indian Ocean, the Arabian Sea and the Red Sea, and the cities where the ship docked along the way included Shanghai, Hong Kong, Penang, Colombo, and Aden. From the Red Sea, the ship traveled through the Suez Canal and entered the Mediterranean Sea to arrive in Marseille. From Marseille, Watsuji traveled to Berlin by train. In addition, while studying in Germany, he traveled not only to various cities in Germany, but also to different parts of Europe including Italy, France, and England.

In this process, he acquired an awareness of the *fudo* of his own country. By engaging with others and by being outside of his own land, he came to the consciousness of the characteristics of his own climate. When imbued with the heat of the Indian Ocean, he came to the awareness of the bone-chilling coldness of the Japanese winter. By being exposed to the care-free clarity of the nature of Italy and Greece, he came to the awareness of the uncontrollable jungles of Japan nurtured by hotness combined with humidity in summer. By experiencing successive fine days in Italy and Greece, Watsuji became aware of the varieties of climatic conditions in Japan: "the cool of a summer's evening, for example, the freshness of the morning, the violent change, sufficient to bring cold at the sunset of an autumn day, the morning cold in winter, enough to shrivel the skin, and, after it, the balmy warmth of an Indian summer day"[42]

As these facts clarify, reflection on the climate of one's own land comes through his or her engagement with other climates. Regarding this process of seeing one's own climate and selfhood by being outside of a given territory, Watsuji wrote, "We ourselves face ourselves in the state of '*ex-sistere*'."[43] Here is an appropriate moment to reflect upon the term '*ex-sistere*,' meaning "standing outside," which was introduced briefly to explain the pervasive nature of a phenomenon such as coldness. As we know, '*ex-sistere*' is a concept in phenomenology that grounds *intentionality*—we don't just think; we always "think of" something. In particular, Watsuji's adoption of the term was influenced by Heidegger's discussion of this idea in *Being and Time* (1927). A passage regarding '*ex-sistere*' from a later writing by Heidegger illuminates the idea in concrete terms:

> If all of us now think, from where we are right here, of the old bridge in Heidelberg, this thinking towards that locale is not a mere experience inside the persons present here; rather, it belongs to the essence of our thinking *of* that bridge that *in itself* thinking *persists* through [durchsteht] the distance to that locale. From this spot right here, we are there at the bridge—we are by no means at some representational content in consciousness. From right here we may even be much nearer to that bridge and to what it makes room for than someone who uses it daily as an indifferent river crossing . . . To say that mortals *are* is to say that *in dwelling* they persist through spaces by virtue of their stay among things and locales. And only because mortals pervade, persist through, spaces by their very essence are they able to go through spaces . . . When 'I' go toward the door of the lecture hall, 'I' am already there, and 'I' could not go to it at all if 'I' were not such that 'I' am there. 'I' am never here only, as this encapsulated body; rather, 'I' am there, that is, 'I' already pervade the space of the room, and only thus can 'I' go through it.[44]

Heidegger distinguished "thinking of" from idealism in which one would cherish an image or representation of what is not physically present. In this process, Heidegger introduced the idea of pervasiveness of the 'I.' Instead of seeing the 'I' as confined within the perimeter of "here and in this body," Heidegger stated a co-presence of the "I of here" and the "I of there." The "I of there" is joined with a thing that is present some distance away, even in a location that is not immediately perceivable. For Heidegger, "thinking of" is thus dependent on the co-presence of the 'I' of here and the 'I' of there, and the co-presence between the 'I' and the thing.

Watsuji's idea of '*ex-sistere*' was influenced by Heidegger's. Watsuji acknowledged '*ex-sistere*' as "the fundamental principle of the structure of ourselves," on which intentionality hinges.[45] Introducing one more time Watsuji's discussion of coldness, he wrote: "when we feel cold, we ourselves are already in the coldness of the outside air."[46] The 'I' that is here and the 'I' that is in the middle of coldness, fashion the formula of reflection in which one sees one's own self. In other words, the discovery of who 'I' am is possible on the basis of me being paradoxically at the outside of the confines of my own selfhood. As explained previously, the same coldness embraces one and another. This means that it is not only the 'I' who is out in the coldness, but others, too. For Watsuji, accordingly, "'*ex-sistere*' is 'to be out among other 'I's'."[47] While the relationship between one and coldness is that of intentionality, the relationship between different 'I's in the coldness is that of mutual compassion. Accordingly, in this process of reflection, an individual's self-discovery is not solitary or self-focused, but becomes part of 'we.' It is we that discover ourselves, not merely fragmented individuals. Watsuji adds that even when one understands reflection "in its visual sense, i.e., if it is understood as to dash against something and rebound from it and to reveal oneself in this rebound or reflection, it can be argued that the word may well indicate the way our selves are exposed to ourselves."[48] Watsuji's trip to the

Indian Ocean created a moment in which he was in the foreign ocean and simultaneously he was from there in his homeland through *thinking of* the homeland. The Watsuji of the Indian Ocean and the Watsuji of the homeland from which he is temporarily dislocated forms the very structure of reflection of his *fudo*.

However, for Watsuji, reflection is not the highest mode of self-apprehension. In self-apprehension, according to Watsuji, our attention is not fixed at ourselves. We do not look merely at our own self. Rather, we reach out to the world. When 'I' find myself feeling cold, this moment of self-apprehension is not an end in itself. Instead, we come to be necessarily connected with *acts* such as looking for more clothes. Consequently, the discovery of one's own self does not confirm the insulated interiority of the subject. Rather, it reconfirms how one is interconnected with the world. "In this self-apprehension," wrote Watsuji, "we are directed to our free creation."[49] More importantly, as argued above, in the phenomenon of self-apprehension in a milieu, the 'I' is joined with other 'I's. In particular, when the tyranny of nature erupts, "we first come to engage ourselves in joint measures to secure early protection from such tyranny."[50] Creations and acts through the joining of different 'I's are the basis for what we call culture. The joining does not indicate only between the 'I' and its contemporaries, but also between the 'I' and the individuals of the past periods. Culture is "an inheritance of self-apprehension accumulated over the years since the time of our ancestors."[51]

It is significant here to mention that coldness is not an isolated phenomenon. Coldness isolated is merely a concept, rather than a climatic phenomenon apprehended in the context of the daily life. Before there is coldness, there is a bone-chilling wind. Coldness is a facet of the wind. Furthermore, a cold wind is, as introduced previously, "experienced as a mountain blast or the cold, dry wind that sweeps through Tokyo at the end of winter."[52] Taking a different example, the heat of summer "wither[s] rich verdure or to entice children to play merrily in the sea."[53] Again, in each of these is the moment of self-discovery. We find ourselves "gladdened or pained . . . in a wind that scatters the cherry blossoms."[54] "In the very heat of summer that scorches down on plants and trees in a spell of dry weather," wrote Watsuji, "we apprehend our wilting selves."[55] We are elements of this tiered system from the abstract to the concrete: from coldness to a cold wind then to a mountain blast and then finally to a mountain blast that makes the human heart bleak. It is important to understand that here the discovery of the self is not the discovery of the subject who feels actively coldness, but the discovery of the self as intermeshed with climatic conditions. In other words, here what one finds is not the heroic subject who centers on an ego to measure the world from the outside, but the self as the capacity to be imbued by the efficacy of climatic phenomena.

5. A Mountain Blast That Makes Our Hearts Bleak
4. A Mountain Blast That Makes My Heart Bleak
3. A Mountain Blast
2. A Cold Wind
1. Coldness

Beyond regional determinism

One would easily think that any study into climatic phenomena of an area and their relationship with a culture takes on the form of a regional determinism. However, Watsuji's *fudo* is a different case. His *fudo* emerged as a reaction against the German *Klimatologie* that operated during the late-eighteenth century and nineteenth century whose concern was how the topographical, geological, flora and fauna of a region define the character of its people and its social reality. For this reason, *Klimatologie* was not just the study of climates, but touched upon the relationship between nature and culture. However, it was still a version of regional determinism.[56] Watsuji took a distinctive approach. In this regard, Nobuo Kioka brings our attention to the subtitle of Watsuji's 1935 publication *Fudo*. Its subtitle, *Study from the Perspective of Humanities* (*ningen teki kousatau*), clarifies that Watsuji's interest was exactly "not that of the ordering of man's life by his natural elements."[57] *Fudo*, or climate, was not merely an environment, but occasioned the mode and structure of the human existence. Watsuji transformed climatic determinism into the ontology of the human being. His study was not merely a version of climatology, but a form of ontology that probes into the spatiality or placed nature of the human being. Watsuji's *fudo* thus makes a significant contribution to the shift in the nature of environmental studies, transcending natural science to espouse ontology as the study of the structure of the human being, in this case, in reference to climate.

As will be discussed in detail later, Watsuji characterized the character of the people in monsoon as receptive and persevering. This should not be seen as a typical case of a climatic determinism, but again be understood from the perspective of ontology. The relationship between monsoon and the character of being receptive and persevering is not that of the first being present first and the second appearing as the result of the first. The two do not exist as separate entities in Watsuji's philosophy, rendering impossible to discuss causality. The relationship between climate as the structural principle of human existence and the character of human beings is that of metaphor. In this relationship, explicating the character of human beings and their cultural expressions by referring to natural phenomena and analogizing nature from culture are equally important, as opposed to regional determinism that flows from climate to the character of a people and then to culture. Watsuji's ultimate proposal is that *fudo* operates as the metaphor of the character of a people. Climate operates as the agency for the people's collective self-awareness. This self-awareness is the basis for the formation of freedom that leads further to creation. Watsuji wrote, again, "We have discovered ourselves in climate, and in this self-apprehension we are directed to our free creation."[58] He further wrote,

> Thus climate is seen to be the factor by which self-active human being can be made objective: climatic phenomena show man how to discover himself as "standing outside" (i.e., '*ex-sistere*'). The self discovered by the cold turns into tools devised against the cold, such as houses or clothes, which then confront the self. Again climate itself, the climate in which we move, and in which we "stand outside," becomes a tool to be used. The cold, for instance, is not only something that sends us off for warm clothes; it can also be utilized to freeze the bean-curd. Heat is not only something that makes us use a fan; it is also the heat that nourishes the rice-plants. Wind has us scurrying to the temple to pray for safety through the typhoon season; it is also the wind that fills a sail. So even in such relationships we "stand outside" in climate and understand ourselves from it, ourselves, that is, as consumers or users. In other words, this self-comprehension through climate at the same time leads us to discover ourselves as confronted with such tools.[59]

In this passage, Watsuji pointed out activity of the human being that uses himself, in conjunction with others, as a tool to cope with, for instance, coldness and that utilizes coldness for a human purpose. At first glance, the activity Watsuji stated of is little difference from the activity that has led us to dig out the earth in order to squeeze out charcoal and oil, in order to cut trees to make paper, and to destruct given topographies in order to erect skyscrapers, apartment complexes and resort facilities. The activity Watsuji endorsed is not the hegemonic activity that is above nature and that transforms nature based upon human wills. Watsuji's activity is necessarily predicated upon the moment of self-awakening. For instance, one awakens into what coldness does by becoming coldness, while the destructive activity is not based upon this kind of self-awakening for its hegemonic, ego-centered and insulated state of the human being. Referring to Kitaro Nishida's (1870-1945) formula, at the basis of this activity is a two-fold structure of the self: the self that is imbued with coldness and the self that sees this self that has been imbued with coldness. The first layer is active, while the second is passive. The first layer is more or less aloof, while the second layer is engaged with the world. These two layers are co-present in order to corroborate the structure of self-awakening in which the 'I' sees the 'I' who has been imbued with coldness. Reflection upon who 'I' am, on one hand, and, on the other, my engagement with the world to the point that my core is filled with coldness are two facets of self-awakening. What Watsuji stated is the fact that this type of self-awakening is the basis for the freedom of human creation beyond his or her being hopelessly governed by natural phenomena.

Accordingly, in Watsuji's manner of thinking, there is room neither for pure freedom nor for complete determinism. Rather, one discovers himself in the coldness that fills his heart, a moment of passivity, and shapes a collective measure to create a warm room, a form of activity. As one has discovered himself that is frozen by coldness, a form of passivity, one utilizes it "to freeze the bean–curd," a form of activity. In any form of act or creation is the moment of self-discovery in reference to a given climatic milieu. Put differently, in any form of activity is the moment of passivity. A different name for this passivity is one's situatedness in the world, in particular, in a climatic milieu. By referring to this process of creation, Watsuji claimed that each of the climatic conditions such as coldness or hotness are not merely terms of natural phenomena, but are inseparably joined with "the way of life,"[60] very much like the coldness that lets the bean–curd be frozen before it is applied to various dishes.

Ethics of the inter-personal

As clarified, for Watsuji, '*ex-sistere*' is "to be out among other 'I's."[61] Climate is by nature the agency of a collective sharing. Climate is the context through which self-enclosed individualism is overcome in favour of an empathy that cultivates collective, cultural measures. *Fudo*, as the spatiality of the human being, is necessarily the space where the presence of the other is acknowledged. Watsuji wrote,

> The problem of climate [*fudo*] affords a pointer for any attempt to analyse the structure of human life. The ontological comprehension of human life is not to be attained by a mere transcendence which regards the structure as one of time, for this has to be transcendence in the sense of the discovery of the self in the other and the subsequent reversal to absolute negation in the union of self and other. In this case, the relationship between man and man must be on a transcendent plane and the relationships themselves, the basis for the discovery of self and other, must already be essentially on a plane which "stands outside" ('*ex-sistere*').[62]

As a matter of fact, for Watsuji, there is never "a man," but men from the beginning. Watsuji thus wrote that the term *man*, the English translation of *ningen*, must be apprehended not as "the individual (anthrōpos, homo, homme, etc.), but man both in [the] individual sense and at the same time man in society, the combination or the association of man."[63] Watsuji's emphasis on the social dimension of the human being is further articulated in his study of ethics. In *Rinrigaku*, his major work on ethics that was first published in 1937, two years after the publication of *Fudo* translated as *A Climate: A Philosophical Study*, Watsuji criticized Western individualism which he accused of substituting the notion of the individual "for the notion of the totality of mankind."[64] In order to solidify his position on the social as the basis for the apprehension of man, Watsuji conducted a philological investigation of *ningen*, or man in the Sino-Japanese linguistic tradition. *Ningen*, or man, is a combination of *nin* and *gen*. *Nin* alone means man, yet is hardly ever used in this singular form to mean man in traditional linguistic usage. *Nin* is always joined with *gen*, an alternative pronunciation of the character *ma* meaning "in-between." *Ningen* thus brings to the notion of man a balanced perspective of the individual and the social.

For Watsuji, individualism is problematic at its core. For instance, the claim of individualism that "the self or the individual is what is disclosed before God, in some cosmic fashion"[65] while excessively criticizing public figures, is flawed in that such individualism paradoxically assumes publicity before God. Watsuji wrote, "In other words, whereas the individual self is hidden from publicity, it is entirely public to the Absolute . . . this means that an individual, in essence, is public."[66] What is taking place in individualism is the preposition of the public nature of the human being before God as her authentic countenance instead of her public nature before other human beings. Further, it is not that the relational dimension of *ma* between man and man is secondary to the individual dimension; Watsuji saw the linguistic construction as indicating that man is fundamentally inscribed with the dimension of 'we.' In fact, Watsuji went so far as to claim that "every trace of the notion of independent existence must be voided."[67] Watsuji further wrote,

> *Ningen* is the public and, at the same time, the individual human beings living within it. Therefore it refers not merely to an individual "human being" nor merely to "society." What is recognized here is a dialectical unity of those double characteristics that are inherent in a human being . . . Oneself and the other are absolutely separated from each other but, nevertheless, become one in communal existence. Individuals are basically different from society and yet dissolve themselves into society. *Ningen* denotes the unity of these contradictories. Unless we keep this dialectical structure in mind, we cannot understand the essence of *ningen*.[68]

In this passage Watsuji raises two dimensions of *ningen* as the dialectical unity of contradictories: One, the relationship between the individual and the social, and the other, the relationship between the individual and another individual. Regarding the first, the two, the individual and the social, are in the relationship of mutual negation. This formula of the mutual negation between the individual and the social is what is lacking in Western theories of sociology.[69] Western sociologies such as Gabriel Tarde's (1843–1904) and George Simmel's (1858–1918) set the individual as the basis, and then emerges the society as the relationship among the "atomic individuals."[70] Or, there is the society first, and then emerges the individuals as defined by the interests of the society. In either case, for Watsuji, the problem lies in the fact that either the individual or the social exists a priori. This priority is nonsensical for him.[71] The individual and the social are mutually dependent on each other. One is not prior to the other.[72] They emerge in simultaneity. Offering a concrete example for how the simultaneity of the relationship operates, Watsuji wrote,

> On the one hand a person exists in a certain role defined for him by his place in his family. But then, on the other hand, he, jointly with his parents and siblings brings into being that relationship called the "family." This being the case, here is a relationship of mutual dependence. The relative positions of parent and child as well as those of elder and younger siblings are defined by relationships in the family; however, the relationships of the family are made between parents and children and between younger and older siblings. These relationships are accepted already as obvious matters of common-sense. For instance, someone without children is never referred to as a "parent." A "parent" can only be so by being a "child's parent." Likewise, a "child" can only be so by being a "parent's child."[73]

The whole cannot sustain itself. It is not substantial like an entity in itself in separation with its parts. It is the parts that substantiate the whole. In turn, the individual does not exist by himself or herself. What makes an individual to be an individual is the whole in which distinctive roles in comparison with other parts are clarified. Accordingly, the individual and the whole "subsist not in themselves, but only in the relationship of each with the other."[74] The whole is like, borrowing Nishida's analogy, a place (*basho*) out of which differences emerge in their particularity and that which joins them into one. The place is productive of opposites, while joining them into one.

The second dimension of *ningen* as the dialectical unity of contradictories concerns itself with the relationship between the individual and another individual. As has been implied, a key to understanding Watsuji's sense of the social is a dialectical structure in which opposite parties are contrastively joined: the father and the mother, the parent and the child, the brother and the sister, and so forth. There is no father unless there is a mother. There is no parent unless there is a child. There is no brother unless there is a sister. One is oneself not because one retains a substantial core in himself or herself, but because of the reciprocity with his or her opposite. For Watsuji, one does not come alone, but emerges necessarily with, and in reference to, the other, realizing the logic of co-dependent origination. Watsuji thus refuted self-sufficiency of a being. The identity of a being is determined not based on what is believed to be existent within itself but based on its dialectical relationship with the opposite. What is seen as internally present in an entity is existent in the first instance because of the external presence of its opposite. The entity and its opposite are intertwined through the principle of inverse correspondence, a higher level of accord that emerges from the disposition of asymmetrical qualities. According to David A. Dilworth, this symmetrical, yet reversed, reciprocity is the logic of "is *and yet* is not" and that of "simultaneity, and bi-conditionality, of opposites without their higher synthesis."[75] This dialectical logic does not indicate a middle ground between two co-emerging identities. This version of dialectic is not "dialectical (sublational) in . . . a Hegelian sense; it does not postulate another level of being or noematic determination."[76] Citing an example, this logic is not meant to synthesize gray out of white and black. This kind of synthesis merely produces another static entity only to lose the creative energy emanating from the juxtaposed, yet inseparable, synthesis of the two opposites. Instead, Watsuji's logic formulates a contradictory synthesis operating on a deeper level of intuition that sees relatedness between contrasting elements.[77]

This dialectical logic is valid not only for individual entities, but also for the identity of regions. In reference to regional identity, as Watsuji's travels to different climates demonstrates, What is significant is to figure out similarity in the pattern between the reflection of one's own self and the reflection of one's own climate. Just as one has to come out of the confine of the

'I' in order to discover who he or she is, Watsuji comes out of his own climate. The self-awareness of the region in which he is situated emerges from the viewpoint of a traveler. The climate of a region is distinctive not because it is self-sufficiently so, but because of its relationship with others. Apprehending the identity of a region in this fashion corresponds to the logic of the dialectics of opposites in which distinctiveness of a climate is not in itself, but rather in its relationship with what it is not. Identity is not something that is present within the interiority of a culture, a land, a people or a territory. Rather, it is a product of a dialectical encounter with others in the form of mutual contrast and dependence. Even when Watsuji's aim was to clarify what his own culture is by referring to the other, what is confirmed here is not necessarily the uniqueness of a culture with a coherent and inherent system of identity, but the dialectical structure of the identity in which one is present because of the other or one comes to be clarified because of its engagement with the other.

Returning to the issue of "in-between," Watsuji's ethics probed further into what gave rise to this betweenness, or that which joins different individuals into one in a dialectical fashion. At this point, Watsuji came to the tradition of the Kyoto philosophical school in which Nishida expounded the idea of nothingness as the true Absolute that gives rise to relatives. The true Absolute for Nishida was not the one that transcends relatives objectively, in which case the Absolute amounts simply becoming another relative, but the one that embraces the relative as its own negation. The true Absolute thus transcends the relatives immanently, since it is intertwined with them through its self-negation.[78] Put differently, in the depth of the individuals is the inscription of nothingness, ontologically open towards the Absolute.[79] Coming very close to Nishida's notion of the relationship between the particular and the universal, Watsuji wrote,

> In this way, the negative structure of a betweenness-oriented being is clarified in terms of the self-returning movement of absolute negativity through its own negation. This is a human being's fundamental structure, which makes its kaleidoscopic appearance in every nook and cranny of a human being. To conceive of the standpoint of a mere individual or of society by itself, while giving no heed to this structure results in an abstraction that brings to light only one aspect of a human being. Indeed, there are three moments that are dynamically unified as the movement of negation: fundamental emptiness, then individual existence, and social existence as its negative development.[80]

The "self-returning movement of absolute negativity," or "the negation of the negation of absolute negativity,"[81] should not be understood as a mythical sublation of the individual into nothingness. It does not "signify a mystical experience in which the individual is immersed in the Absolute."[82] Rather, the sublation (*Aufheben*) takes on the form of participating in the socio-ethical whole in various forms of family, mates of different groups, a corporation, a state and so forth.[83] The destination of the self-returning movement of the Absolute is not fixed, but is open towards possibilities of the human socio-ethical relationships. For this reason, for Watsuji, "the movement of the negation of absolute negativity is said to be the law of human beings; that is, it is ethics."[84] The way an individual relates himself or herself to the Absolute is not direct, but is conducted through taking part in the socio-ethical whole. In this regard, the path back to the Absolute was exemplified by great religious figures such as Jesus and Buddha who stayed with other human beings in the field of the daily life after the enlightenment. The enlightenment into emptiness is thus necessarily joined with "compassion" towards other human beings, realizing one's absolute reliance on God through the form of love. For Watsuji, this compassionate relation indicates not a unity between object and object but "act-connections between person and person like communication or association, in which persons as subjects concern themselves with each other."[85] Watsuji was thus critical of mysticism and Hinayana Buddhism in that it is one's return to the Absolute to be a personal matter, depriving compassion towards other fellow human beings.[86]

Inter-*fudos* and the subject transcending the insularity of a *fudo*

It seems, however, that this ethics of the whole by Watsuji needs to be taken with caution. On the one hand, Watsuji seems to interpret the human relationship based upon the logic of the contrasted inter-dependence. At the level of the family, opposites are dependent on each other: father and mother, brother and sister, parents and children, and so forth. For Watsuji, one is there because of the other. One would not be present, if it were not for the other. His reading of the Japanese climate also reflected this manner of thinking. "The bamboo . . . covered in snow" was a scene characteristic of Japan integrating a woody plant of a tropical belt with icy crystals of a frigid zone. This climatic phenomenon embodies a contrasted balance between opposites. This pattern of thinking continued in his ethics. The earlier quotes from the 1949 edition of his ethics regarding the criticism of individualism, as we have seen, eventually put emphasis upon mutual negation between the individual and society.

On the other hand, it is sometimes unclear whether Watsuji made the whole absolute to the point that the individuality of a person is subsumed. In *Fudo*, Watsuji wrote, "The virtue that is called filial piety from the aspect of the household becomes loyalty from the standpoint of the state. So filial piety and loyalty are essentially identical, the virtue prescribing the individual in accordance with the interests of the whole."[87] As introduced above, he also saw the "house" in Japan as "[evincing] most starkly the fact that the family as a whole takes precedence over its individual members."[88] He came dangerously close to promoting imperialism by relying on the analogy of the house, transforming his dialectical logic into the logic of totality sacrificing individuals. Watsuji equated filial piety with one's loyalty towards the emperor and the imperial family. Lacking respect of the individuals, individuals are rendered into a means to achieve the agenda of the emperor acknowledged as the unchallengeable father. The whole that is composed of contrasting differences is replaced by the whole as the superior that governs the subordinates such as the emperor over the subjects, the master over the disciples, the parents and the children, and the elder over the young, approximating his logic to the Confucian dualistic hierarchy. This logic of totality hidden in Watsuji's philosophy is particularly troublesome in that Watsuji was in a tacit support of the Imperial system. Berque connects this logic of totality with the logic of the predicate that characterizes leading thinkers of Japan such as Nishida. Berque claims that in the process in which the subject is subsumed to the predicate, the particularity of the subject is utterly put aside.[89]

The historical mapping also reinforces an accusation of nationalism on Watsui's philosophy. His discussion of the filial piety, along with his illumination of the sophistication and elegance of the Japanese art in confrontation with Dilthey's orientalist characterization, came at a moment when general spirit of nationalism was surging. Not to mention the then increasingly militaristic atmosphere, in the area of art, the rediscovery of Japanese tradition was conducted in a nationalistic fashion by Japanese Romanticism. Japanese Romanticism, a movement in literature, operated from the 1930s to the end of World War II, under the leadership of Yojuro Yasuda (1910–81), supporting consciously or unconsciously the uniqueness and superiority of Japanese culture. For instance, *Wabi*, "an aesthetic and moral principle [in tea ceremony] advocating the enjoyment of a quiet, leisurely life free from worldly concerns," was beautifully elaborated by such writers as Kakuzo Okakura (1862–1913), the author of *The Book of Tea* (1906), *The Ideals of the East* (1903), and *The Awakening of Japan* (1904). *Sabi* and *susabi*, the medieval aesthetic notions cultivated by Basho (1644–94) through the literary form of *Haikai*, were rediscovered and classicized by Japanese Romantic writers and critics such as Yasuda, Yoshinori Onishi (1888–1959), the author of *The Theory of Fuga: A Study of "Sabi"* (*Fuga-ron Sabi no Kenkyu*) (1940), and Okazaki Yoshie (1892–1982), the author of *The Tradition of Beauty* (*Bi no dento*) (1940). The aesthetics of *yami*, or darkness, was articulated in Junichiro Tanizaki's (1886–1965) *In Praise of Shadow*. In short, the Japanese romantics strove to clarify the distinctive characteristics of Japanese culture by looking into the literary and artistic sources of the medieval and Edo periods. Watsuji's positive and even proud evaluation of the Japanese tradition during the 1930s and 1940s must be seen as symptomatic of this romantic tendency to a degree at least.

However, one cannot simply blame even pre-war Watsuji as nationalistic in the same vein as, for instance, Yasuda was. This is because, even in his *Fudo*, a representative pre-war writing in his corpus, Watsuji's method of comparison between the Japanese culture and other cultures was not unfair. In order to figure out the unique nature of Watsuji's comparative method, I would first like to clarify how different his method was from the way Japanese Romanticism utilized comparison. Japanese Romanticism adopted the method of comparison in their writings as the way of proving the superiority of the Japanese culture. For instance, Yasuda's comparison of Japanese bridges with their Western counterparts is a good example. In his criticism of Yasuda's study of the Japanese bridge as uncovered in the classical literary context, Daniel C. Strack, a literary critic, convincingly illustrates that "Yasuda's . . . sweeping study, *Bridges of Japan*, while portending to be a comparative essay, only mentions a handful of foreign bridges and offers not a single example of a non-Japanese bridge in literary context."[90] Yasuda exemplified the heavy masonry bridges built by the Romans and the iron bridges constructed during Napoleon's era to support his claim of the culturally crude militaristic dimension of the Western culture, and, by contrast, to highlight the refined and sophisticated artistic sensitivity of Japan with the image of loving peace. Any particularity of the Japanese bridge that might emerge from a comparison with the unjustly selected Western examples, transforms into the uniqueness of Japan, and eventually her cultural superiority. Yasuda's literary study was, in this perspective, just another example of inseparably consolidated nationalism and aestheticism, a trend that had characterized pre-war Japanese aesthetics since its formation during the late nineteenth century. Yasuda's seemingly pure essay on the Japanese bridge in literary context did not illuminate the purity of an artifact as a form of criticism against society in which the inability of artists and intellectuals in changing the course of history led them to secure a space for self-propitiation in art.[91] Nor did it have any dimension of the purely formalistic experimentation that would refute art that has become the deceptive self-reflection of a political ideology.[92] Yasuda's essay dealt not with the bridge itself as a valuable, trans-national construction of all human cultures, but with the "Japanese bridge." The lack of a trans-national dimension necessarily imbued his starting point with a nationalistic tinge.

Then how was Watsuji's comparison different? In this regard, it is worth introducing Kioka's interpretation. Kioka acknowledges that, as Berque argues, Watsuji's theory of climate lacks objectivity in that his personal experience became the characteristic of a climate. Despite this problem, one significant point about Watsuji's study of different climates is that it was nomadic (Figures 1.2, 1.3, 1.4). This nomadic nature of his theory of climate is expressed in the form of analogy between the climates and the characters of peoples, formulating a proportional relationship among different climates. The reason why Japan is often mentioned in his study is because of his familiarity with Japan, not necessarily because of his nationalistic partiality. Most importantly, Watsuji's theory of climate entails a unique type of subject, which Kioka names the subject of "inter-*fudo*s (*kanfudosei*)."[93] It is a subject that stands in the interstitial zone between different *fudo*s (here I am rendering *fudo* plural to follow the convention of English). In this type of subjectivity, the discovery of who 'I' am is conducted upon the encounter with the other. The Watsuji of the Arabian Desert discovers his non-desert nature as a monsoon person whose identity Watsuji had not felt before. In this context emerges a proportional formulation:

Monsoon: Submissive and Persevering = Desert: Confrontational and Willful

For Kioka, this analogical relationship overcomes any possibility of making absolute a climate and its cultural expression absolute. Furthermore, the analogy is an open one, accepting pairs of particulars. For instance,

Monsoon: Submissive and Persevering = Desert: Confrontational and Willful = Meadow: Rational and Regular

For this open analogy, for Kioka, Watsuji's *fudo* is not self-centered, but moves along "the logic of particularization" in which both the 'I' and the other are rendered relative. The subject of "inter-*fudo*s" assumes a position that is neither a center, nor a periphery, reflecting the nature

FIGURE 1.2 Landscape of monsoon (photo by author)

FIGURE 1.3   Landscape of desert (photo by Sungwoo Ahn, courtesy of the photographer)

of analogy that does not presume the particular under universality and that moves from a particularity to another particularity. In the case of empathy, there still exists a privileged center. It is still self-centered. It places one's subjective consciousness at the center and then enters the interiority of the other and understands the other by projecting what is present in one's interiority. This is a closed analogy that is predicated upon the fixed and centralized image of the self. In contrast, Watsuji's logic is that of discovering the other in a climatic context and discovering one's own self by taking the other as the mirror against which who 'I' am is reflected. It is the logic of mutual discovery between who 'I' am and who he is. Kioka does acknowledge that Watsuji was in support of imperialism. Yet, he discovers the logic of particularization from Watsuji's theory. In addition, Watsuji's logic is not merely a logic, but ethics of de-centralization to overcome self-centeredness. Watsuji's logic is a post-colonial logic in that modernity placed Europe as the center and other parts of the world as peripheries, and peripheries were then conquered and subjected to the center. In contrast, Watsuji's logic is the logic of de-centralization, proliferating particulars and their proportional, yet contrasted, reciprocities.[94]

Extending the significance of Watsuji's *fudo*, Kioka differentiates between the communal and the public. The communal is fundamentally based upon the fact that one is born in a land to which he and others belong together. A typical form of the communal is a village. This *Gemeinschaft* was the primary subject of study in climatology, as there is a close bond between the land, on one hand, and, on the other, the industry, eatery and culture. The communal is sustained often by internal rules of operation such as a hierarchy, placing primarily the whole such as the family over the individuals and the village over the villagers.

FIGURE 1.4 Landscape of meadow (photo by author)

In contrast, the public occurs at a moment when one seeks to move beyond the land and its correlate society. It is a turning away from the protected interiority of the communal. The one who leaves the communal is the one who has awakened to the presence of the exterior, placing one in a dynamic between belonging to a communal society and being free to come out of the society. The public thus lives on the volition to place oneself beyond the territory. Watsuji's subject of inter-*fudo*s is exactly this type of subject who stands in a public sphere. He or she is the one who negates the centralizing desire, who overcomes self-centeredness, and who finally moves into the interstitial space between different communities. He or she expands his or her horizon not by negating the other, but by negating his or her own self. This public sphere is called by Kioka, the place of nothingness, where our conventional interests in the identities of groups are overcome to face an individual as an individual. It is not a place of loneliness, but a place where self-awareness in the form of (de-centralized) one seeing one's own self as a person belonging to a particular *fudo* is carried out. It is also a place where a de-centralized individual encounters another de-centralized individual to experiment unconditioned possibilities and potentialities that may exist in the inter-personal to formulate an alternative society. For Kioka, this de-centralizing logic of particularization and its correlate interstitial space of self-discovery and of the inter-personal encounter is Watsuji's most significant contribution.[95]

Notes

1 Watsuji's relationship with German thinkers is especially important in apprehending the cultural background for his philosophy. One could list, for instance, Raphel von Koeber (1843–1924) from whom

Watsuji learned the hermeneutics of Friedrich Scheleiermacher (1768–1834), as well as Immanuel Kant's (1724–1804) and Georg Wilhelm Friedrich Hegel's (1770–1831) idealism, and Wilhelm Dilthey (1833–1911) whom Watsuji criticized for Dilthey's orientalist position. Graham Mayeda, *Time, Space and Ethics in the Philosophy of Watsuji Tetsuro, Kuki Shuzo, and Martin Heidegger*, New York, London: Routledge, 2006, p. 6; Tetsuro Watsuji, *A Climate: A Philosophical Study*, trans. Geoffrey Bownas, Ministry of Education Printing Bureau, 1961, p. 171.

2 Ibid., p. 5.

3 Tetsuro Watsuji, *A Climate: A Philosophical Study*, trans. Geoffrey Bownas, Ministry of Education Printing Bureau, 1961, preface, v.

4 Tetsuro Watsuj, *Watsuji Tetsuro's Rinrigaku Ethics in Japan*, trans. Yamamoto Seisaku and Robert E. Carter, Albany: State University of New York, 1996, p. 174.

5 Ibid., p. 173.

6 Ibid., p. 174.

7 Ibid.

8 Ibid.

9 Ibid.

10 Ibid.

11 Ibid.

12 Tetsuro Watsuji, *A Climate: A Philosophical Study*, p. 1.

13 Ibid., p. 5.

14 Ibid.

15 Ibid., p. 14.

16 Ibid., p. 16.

17 Ibid., pp. 39–40.

18 Augustin Berque, "The Ontological Structure of Mediance as a Ground of Meaning in Architecture," in *Structure and Meaning in Human Settlements*, eds Tony Atkin and Joseph Rykwert, Philadelphia: University of Pennsylvania Museum of Archaeology and Anthropology, 2005, p. 98.

19 According to Berque, the Western perspective of the world was in general in refusal of the realm of trajection, Plato's banning of the poets being symbolic of the very tendency. The limit of the Western thinking based upon reason and its correlate formal logic consists in the clear division between the subject who utters a predication and the subject of which the predication is made. It thus fails to admit the zone of tetralemmas in which the first and the second are intertwined. Criticizing this Western logic that opened a space for pure reason and natural science, Berque brought to attention the logic of the middle ground such as Nagarjuna's that acknowledges a realm in which A and not-A are corresponding to each other. It is a zone of symbolicity that transcends the dualism between the subject and object. Augustin Berque, "The Ontological Structure of Mediance as a Ground of Meaning in Architecture," p. 100.

20 Ibid., p. 98.

21 Ibid., p. 99.

22 Tetsuro Watsuji, *A Climate: A Philosophical Study*, p. 4.

23 Ibid., p. 135.

24 Ibid., p. 200.

25 Ibid.

26 Ibid., p. 198.

27 Ibid.

28 Ibid., p. 199.

29 Ibid., p. 200.

30 Ibid.

31 Ibid., p. 135.

32 Ibid., p. 134.

33 Ibid., p. 201.

34 Ibid., p. 203.

35 Ibid.

36 Ibid.

37 Ibid., p. 135.

38 Ibid., pp. 137–8.

39 Ibid., p. 202.

40 Ibid., p. 137.
41 Ibid., p. 171.
42 Ibid., p. 200.
43 Ibid., p. 3.
44 Martin Heidegger, "Building, Dwelling, Thinking," in *Basic Writings*, ed. David Farrell Krell, San Francisco: HarperSanFrancisco, 1993, pp. 358–9 (Heidegger's italicizations).
45 Tetsuro Watsuji, *A Climate: A Philosophical Study*, p. 4.
46 Ibid., p. 3.
47 Ibid., p. 4.
48 Ibid., p. 3.
49 Ibid., p. 6.
50 Ibid.
51 Ibid.
52 Ibid.
53 Ibid.
54 Ibid.
55 Ibid.
56 Nobuo Kioka, *Fudo no ronri: chiri tetsugaku eno michi*, Kyoto: Minerubashobo, 2011, p. 8.
57 Tetsuro Watsuji, *A Climate: A Philosophical Study*, p. v.
58 Ibid., p. 6.
59 Ibid., p. 12.
60 Ibid., p. 134.
61 Ibid., p. 4.
62 Ibid., p. 12.
63 Ibid., p. 8.
64 Tetsuro Watsuji, *Watsuji Tetsuro's Rinrigaku, Ethics in Japan*, trans. Yamamoto Seisaku and Robert E. Carter, Albany, NY: State University of New York Press, 1996, p. 9.
65 Ibid., p. 146.
66 Ibid.
67 According to William LaFleur, who situated Watsuji's ethical thinking within the Mahayanan Buddhist tradition of emptiness, this rejection of the priority of the individual to create a dialectic between the individualistic and the societal and relational aspect of the human being bases its ground upon Nagarjuna's idea of "co-dependent origination." William LaFleur, "Buddhist Emptiness in the Ethics and Aesthetics of Watsuji Tetsuro," *Religious Studies* 14 (2): 245–7; Tetsuro Watsuji, *Rinrigaku*, vol. 1, Tokyo: Iwanami shoten, 1963, p. 107 (LaFleur's translation).
68 Tetsuro Watsuji, *Watsuji Tetsuro's Rinrigaku, Ethics in Japan*, p. 15.
69 Watsuji wrote,

> A grasp of man's two sided nature—that is, as individual and as society—and the discovery of man's deepest essence in this double dimension never even comes up for discussion when it has already been assumed that a clear distinction between man and society is to be part of the very definition of terms.

Tetsuro Watsuji, *Rinrigaku*, vol. 1, p. 16; William LaFleur, "Buddhist Emptiness in the Ethics and Aesthetics of Watsuji Tetsuro," p. 243.
70 Tetsuro Watsuji, *Watsuji Tetsuro's Rinrigaku, Ethics in Japan*, p. 105.
71 Watsuji wrote,

> Man's existence in relationships is an existence which comprises both the individual and society through mutual negation. Therefore, human existence cannot be explained as a situation in which we first have individuals and then establishment of relationships among them; nor can it be explained as first a society and then the emergence of individuals out of that society. In both of these explanations it is the "priority" which is the impossibility.

Tetsuro Watsuji, *Rinrigaku*, vol. 1, p. 107; William LaFleur, "Buddhist Emptiness in the Ethics and Aesthetics of Watsuji Tetsuro," p. 245.

72 Tetsuro Watsuji, *Rinrigaku*, vol. 1, p. 59; William LaFleur, "Buddhist Emptiness in the Ethics and Aesthetics of Watsuji Tetsuro," p. 244.
73 Tetsuro Watsuji, *Rinrigaku*, vol. 1, p. 59; William LaFleur, "Buddhist Emptiness in the Ethics and Aesthetics of Watsuji Tetsuro," pp. 243–4.
74 Tetsuro Watsuji, *Watsuji Tetsuro's Rinrigaku, Ethics in Japan*, p. 101.
75 David A. Dilworth, Introduction and Postscript in Kitaro Nishida, *Last Writings: Nothingness and the Religious Worldview*, trans. David A. Dilworth, Honolulu: University of Hawaii Press, 1987, pp. 5–6, pp. 130–1.
76 Ibid.
77 Although Watsuji was only tangentially related to the Kyoto Philosophical School led by Kitaro Nishida, this manner of thinking, the logic of contrasted interdependence, was a unique aspect of the School. Nishida, in his theory, challenged the 'I' as a never-doubted *a priori* category. In contrast, breaking the pre-conceived solidity of the 'I,' Nishida introduced the subjectivity of "the non-I"—sometimes called "the ego-less I"—from which the 'I' as the subject emerges. "The non-I" is nothingness or emptiness. It is the horizon where the confrontation between being and non-being is transcended in favor of their co-emergence. Overcoming the idea of the universal as the abstracted denominator of things, Nishida articulated emptiness as the concrete universal from which the individual differences emerge in their unmitigated particularity. This emptiness, the ultimate *eidos*, was a topos in which beings emerge, exist and evaporate. Kitaro Nishida, *Fundamental Problems of Philosophy, the World of Action and the Dialectical World*, trans. David A. Dilworth, Tokyo: Sophia University, 1970, p. 22; Kitaro Nishida, *Art and Morality*, trans. David A. Dilworth and Valdo H. Viglielmo, Honolulu: University of Hawaii Press, 1973, pp. 18–19; Kitaro Nishida, *Complete Works (Nishida Kitaro zenshu)*, Tokyo: Iwanami shoten, 1947, vol. 4, pp. 217–19, pp. 229–31.
78 Nishida developed an ingenious logic of the predicate that is intertwined with the particular through its own self-negation. Being a productive vector, the predicate causes the subject to come into being by negating itself on its own accord, yet only in temporality, as it obliterates what has been predicated in order to redeem its own self-possession. The self-affirmation and self-determination of the universal is necessarily conjoined with the subsequent negation of what it has predicated of itself by articulating itself into the realm of particulars, negation indicating self-demise for the particulars, yet with the promise of their unification with the universal. Nishida's logic of the predicate holds together these two irreconcilable and opposing directions in absolute contradiction. This kind of predicate is the true predicate for Nishida, since it transcends the self not objectively, but immanently, and since it is intermeshed with the self through its self-negation. If the Absolute transcends the relative objectively, it would merely end up becoming another relative, no matter how extensive and inclusive it might be. The true Absolute is that which includes within itself its own negation as the way to be related and connected to the relative. Kitaro Nishida, *Last Writings: Nothingness and the Religious Worldview*, Honolulu: University of Hawaii, 1987, pp. 72–8, 100.
79 Robert E. Carter stated of this horizon as the true authentic ground of the human being:

> True *authenticity* is not the asserting of one's individuality, as with the Existentialists, but an annihilation of the self such that one is now identified with others in a non-dualistic merging of the self and other. Now there is only the authenticity of benevolence or compassion, which is the "authentic countenance" of *ningen* . . . The answer is that we, and all other things, already were as that faceless, distinctionless, thingless *nothingness* out of which all things as distinct emerge and that is the ground of all distinctions, yet that itself is without distinction. This is our "authentic home ground." . . . Just as the movement of negation was, in its extreme, the self-activity of absolute negativity, so temporality is precisely the manner in which absolute negativity exhibits itself. That is to say, an established betweenness is, in its extreme, the absolute wholeness that consists of the nonduality of the self and the other; that is, the authentic countenance prior to the birth of one's parents, as is said in Zen Buddhism. In other words, it is authenticity as the ground out of which we, fundamentally speaking, come forth.

> Tetsuro Watsuji, *Watsuji Tetsuro's Rinrigaku Ethics in Japan*, p. 187; Robert E. Carter, "Interpretive Essay: Strands of Influence," p. 332.

80 Tetsuro Watsuji, *Watsuji Tetsuro's Rinrigaku, Ethics in Japan*, p. 117.
81 Ibid., p. 121.
82 Ibid.
83 Ibid.
84 Ibid.
85 Watsuji's discussion of the social, or the socio-ethical whole, is characterized by the logic of interdependent opposites between a person and a person. Watsuji saw this point as differentiating his position from that of Heidegger. Heidegger's *Dasein* transfers the concept of intentionality to the relationship between man and tools, moving towards the world away from the subjective consciousness. According to Watsuji, however, in spite of Heidegger's denial, Heidegger veils the primary relationship between person and person in the process of bringing forward the relationship between man and tool. Heidegger's disciple Karl Löwith clarified the meaning of the world as the relationship between person and person, instead of dealing with individual persons. Watsuji wrote, "Here, a human being is a person 'together with others,' and the world is *mit-Welt*, that is, the public whereas *being in the world* means 'to relate with others.'" Ibid., pp. 17–18.
86 Ibid., p. 123.
87 Tetsuro Watsuji, *A Climate: A Philosophical Study*, p. 148.
88 Ibid., p. 141.
89 Nobuo Kioka, *Fudo no ronri: chiri tetsugaku eno michi*, pp. 13–15.
90 Daniel C. Strack, "Nihon no hashi to sekai no hashi: Yasuda Yojuro to Yanakita Kunio ni okeru 'hashi' no isou," *Kitakyushu University Faculty of Humanities Journal*, vol. 61 (2001): 1–15.
91 The society in which Japanese artists and writers were practicing art during the pre-war period was characterized by ultra-nationalism. Here, I find it useful to reflect upon the relationship between art and a dominant ideology of a society, a theme discussed by many art critics such as Peter Burger and Clement Greenberg (1909–94). In his *Theory of the Avant-Garde*, Burger claimed that when art has become the objectification of dominant ideologies of a society and a vehicle to propagandize them, a different form of art emerges in order to criticize such art and to experimental values opposing the ideologies. In a similar fashion, Greenberg argued that the avant-garde movement is the very reflection of the instinct of self-preservation in order to keep the value of art in the midst of ideological confusion and culture industry. Greenberg stated that the task of the avant-garde is "to perform in opposition to bourgeois society the function of finding new and adequate cultural forms for the expression of that same society." Therefore, the autonomous aspect of avant-garde art is achieved by art's complete detachment from bourgeois society. A Bohemia is considered by the avant-garde artists to be a sanctuary emancipated from the governing ideologies of the society. This complex relationship between the avant-garde and a dominant ideology of a society has relevance to the discussion of the role and position of the artists during the ultra-nationalistic period in Japan. While a precise evaluation of the role and position goes beyond the capacity of this study, the issue hinges on whether the artists distanced themselves from the ideology or served it consciously or unconsciously with their works. Peter Burger, *Theory of the Avant-Garde*, trans. Michael Shaw, Minneapolis: University of Minnesota Press, 1984, pp. 47–9; Clement Greenberg, "Towards a Newer Laocoon," in *Clement Greenberg: The Collected Essays and Criticism*, ed. John O'Brian, Chicago: University of Chicago Press, 1986, pp. 23–37; T.J. Clark, "Clement Greenberg's Theory of Art," *Critical Inquiry*, vol. 9, n. 1 (Sept. 1982), pp. 139–56.
92 According to Greenberg's view of the autonomy of art, art's detachment from the praxis of life, i.e., the ideological confusion and culture industry prospering in bourgeois society, leads art to conduct an aesthetic attempt to eliminate the subject matter from the work. This is because the subject matter has extrinsic value borrowed from the life field of the bourgeois society and is thus impure. Conversely, form of the work strikes the avant-garde artists as the pure, autonomous and absolute aspect of art. Greenberg states that "content is to be dissolved so completely into form that the work of art or literature cannot be reduced in whole or in part to anything not itself." The artist's concern about form of the work develops further into

the artist's attention to the medium, or the materialistic base for the art. Clement Greenberg, "Towards a Newer Laocoon," p. 39; Clement Greenberg, "Avant-Garde and Kitsch," in *Clement Greenberg: The Collected Essays and Criticism*, ed. John O'Brian, Chicago: University of Chicago Press, 1986, pp. 5–22.

93 Nobuo Kioka, *Fudo no ronri: chiri tetsugaku eno michi*, Kyoto: Minerubashobo, 2011, pp. 319–23.
94 Ibid., pp. 319–20.
95 Ibid., p. 312.

2

"SELF-LESS OPENNESS" AND *FUDO*

Renewed sustainable significance of Japanese vernacular architecture

A probe into the linkage between Tetsuro Watsuji's (1889–1960) notion of *fudo* and concrete architectural practice is aided by Watsuji himself. Watsuji not only reflected upon *fudo*, its relationship with "who we are," and its inter-personal ethics, but also wrote of the characteristics of the spatial configuration of traditional Japanese housing in reference to *fudo*. His insightful account of the configuration contrasted itself effectively with the evaluation of the Japanese house made by Westerners and Japanese architects. As a matter of fact, the architects critical of the traditional Japanese configuration were quite swift in steering its transformation to suit the ideology of individualism with an emphasis on privacy, as well as to ensure efficiency of circulation and functional clarity. Despite being a contemporary to these architects, Watsuji's position was nearly opposite to them; he refreshed the significance of the spatial configuration of the Japanese house from the perspective of *fudo* and of its inter-personal basis, criticizing individualism and its concomitant spatiality.

Criticism of the traditional Japanese house

The discourse on how to reform traditional Japanese houses was formulated by Japanese who studied in the West and by foreigners who were living in Japan. In 1898, "How to reform the house (*kaokukairyoudan*)" was serially published in *Jijishinpou*, a newspaper launched in 1882, a total of 29 times (Figure 2.1). The traditional Japanese house was criticized for three reasons: first, noise; second, the lack of clarity in the functional definition of the rooms; and third, interruption of privacy, as one has to go through different rooms in order to move from one part of the house to another.[1] The counterpart against which the Japanese house was measured was the Western masonry house, with a clear division between the corridor and the rooms. The Western house does not suffer from noise, as the walls were thick, solid and fixed. The rooms are functionally clear—kitchen, dining, bedrooms, living room and so forth. Each room has a single door leading to a corridor, through which one can reach another room without intervening into any other. In contrast, the traditional Japanese house leaves much to be desired in these three aspects. The partition was found too flimsy and acoustically defective. Each room is used in one way or another, lacking designation in terms of usage. A room is directly interconnected with another without the mediation of a passageway, blemishing completely its independence.

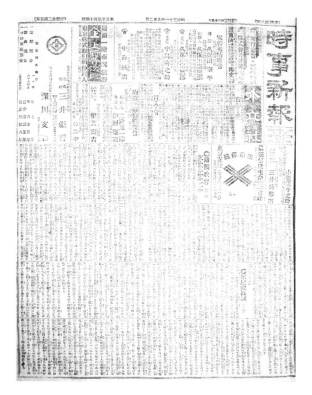

FIGURE 2.1 "How to reform the house (*kaokukairyoudan*)," *Jijishinpou*, Friday 2, September, 1898

These three aspects guided the transformation of the Japanese house. In particular, the second and third aspects paved a way to the modification of the Japanese house without a corridor to one with a corridor. Regarding the second aspect, the criticism was targeted first at the mixture between dining and other collective activities of the family in the same room. The subsequent demand to reserve a separate space for dining had the effect of solidifying the status of another room where collective activities of the family other than dining could take place—the living room. This room designed not with *tatami* mats but with sofas, chairs, a low table and a fireplace to follow the Western style of living emerged as the new core for the domestic life. In appearance, the living room-centered house was family-oriented, as it positioned the communal space at the center. This appearance was, however, misleading to a degree. Designation of a living room was a compromising solution for collectivity in a domestic space with intensified privacy, which the self-enclosed rooms with fixed walls embodied. At any rate, thanks to the centrality of the living room, any traffic from one room to another is led to the living room through a corridor (except in the case where the parents in the master bedroom approach the infant's quarter directly for immediate attention through a supplementary door). The division of functions—the living room, the kitchen, the dining room, individual rooms for parents and individuals—contributed to the removal of interruptions and is subsequently intertwined with the issue of securing privacy for each room. A common device that was essential for both functional clarity and privacy was the corridor.

One figure who led the discourse on the corridor was Junkichi Tanabe (1879–1926). His position was radical. He believed in utilizing the model of the Western Australian bungalow in order to reshape the spatial structure of the Japanese house (Figure 2.2). He brought to attention two aspects of the Australian house: first, the roofed verandas both in front of the house and at the back; and second, the central corridor along which rooms are lined up. Tanabe claimed that the roofed veranda was equivalent to the *engawa*, the Japanese veranda that stands between rooms and the garden, and it is suitable for the hot Japanese summer. After pointing out this similarity between the Japanese house and its Australian counterpart, he advocated implementing a central corridor within the Japanese house, as it would eliminate the problem of going through different rooms, and secure independence for each room. His introduction of the Australian house in this

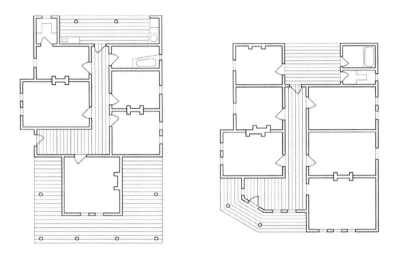

FIGURE 2.2 Junkichi Tanabe (1879–1926), plan, Western Australian bungalow (redrawn by Dasoul Park based upon Seijou Uchida, Mitsuo Ookawa and Youetsu Hujiya, eds, *Kindainihonjuutakushi*, Tokyo: Kajimashuppankai, 2008, p. 40)

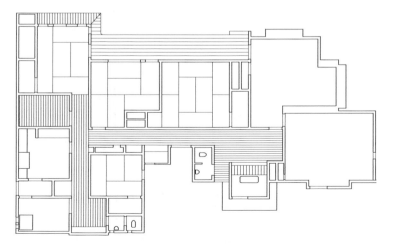

FIGURE 2.3 Arata Endō (1889–1951), proposal of a middle-class house (redrawn by Dasoul Park based upon Seijou Uchida, Mitsuo Ookawa and Youetsu Hujiya, eds, *Kindainihonjuutakushi*, Tokyo: Kajimashuppankai, 2008, p. 54)

way facilitated a shift towards the espousal of a central corridor in Japan. Several years later, a proposal for middle-class housing made by Arata Endō (1889–1951) at the occasion of the Home Fair (*Katei hakurankai*) organized by *Kokuminshinbun*, a newspaper company, had corridors that allowed independent accesses to rooms of *tatami* mats (Figure 2.3). Emphasis was placed on the formulation of uninterrupted procession from the entrance to any part of the house by devising a system of a central corridor. Additional features of the house included fixed walls between Japanese rooms, as well as Western rooms near the entrance that functioned as a guest reception and library.

Corridor and individualism

The house with a corridor in the middle—the feature seen by the Japanese as typical of Western houses—was in fact a historical product. The private house as we know it today grew in Europe and colonial New England during the seventeenth century. Its development came with a specific class and political connotation, as it was intended to suit the bourgeoisie in Europe and the middle class in the United States. For instance, during the medieval period, town houses were developed as "not only the family home," but also "a manufacturing locale, counting house, store, or shop."[2] They sheltered not only the owner and his family, but also relatives, employees, apprentices and guests. Separation of rooms for separate activities was unusual, as "inhabitants lived, slept and ate in large, open halls that accommodated different functions principally by the rearrangement of furniture."[3] During the Renaissance, the medieval-style halls were still favored even by aristocratic families. It was at the beginning of the seventeenth century that the presence of the public from the home started to be gradually abolished.[4]

Robin Evans' (1944–93) study of the tally between the portrayal of human figures and the architectural plan from Mannerism to the early twentieth century is particularly enlightening here. For instance, in Raphael's (1483–1520) paintings drawn during his later period, such as *Madonna dell'Impannata* (1514), the depicted figures do not occupy compartmentalized, geometrical and static locations, but are overlapped. They "grasp, embrace, hold and finger each other's bodies as if their recognition rested more firmly on touch than on sight."[5] This "web of linked embraces and gestures"[6] was also a principle upon which Raphael practiced architecture. A good

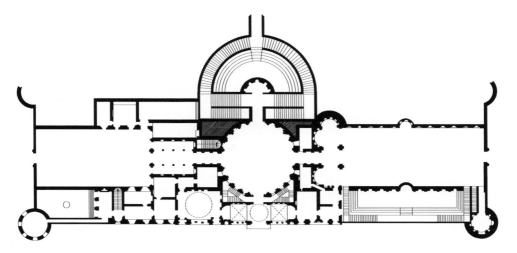

FIGURE 2.4   Raphael (1483–1520), Villa Madama (1525) (redrawn by Seho Kee based upon Robin Evans, *Translations from Drawing to Building*, Cambridge, MA: MIT Press, 1997, p. 61)

example was Villa Madama (1525). The plan as proposed by the earliest surviving plan (Figure 2.4) integrates the axial and symmetrical composition with a circular court and a grand loggia over-looking a garden, on one hand, and on the other, a non-axial, non-hierarchical disposition of rooms. Around the court are chambers of various sizes and shapes, with no clear division between the corridor and the chambers. One chamber is never identical to any other. It fills in the site by joining itself with others in a way that defies any manifest logic. Traversing the house thus meant going through different rooms. The whole emerges as "an accumulation of these enclosures"[7] and "a matrix of discrete but thoroughly interconnected chambers."[8] One room is directly con-nected to another, having multiple doors, not just one.[9] If the movement along the courtyard and the garden is axial and processional, the movement that occurs behind the courtyard is a roaming-around, intersecting accidentally with the paths of others. The configuration was governed not by the compositional transparency, but by the style of life in which the members of the family, the guests and even the servants were allowed to intermingle. In short, the configuration embodied "fondness for company, proximity and incident."[10]

According to Evans, it is only in the early part of the nineteenth century that the room with more than one door would be considered ill-designed. The house composed of such rooms—"thoroughfare rooms"—would be inconvenient, as it would not provide any moment of retreat or retirement.[11] What was inseparably conjoined with the evolution of the rooms with only one door was the development of a planning maneuver that would guarantee minimized contacts between the members of the household. The ploy was none other than the corridor, forming a clear distinction between the passageway and the spaces that can be occupied.[12] As a matter of fact, the corridor itself, according to Evans' research, makes its first appearance in 1597 in England and grew into a version that meets the contemporary conception of the cor-ridor during the second third of the seventeenth century (Figure 2.5). Of course, the initial motive to devise a corridor was class-related: this device prevented servants from appearing in the spaces meant to be occupied by other individuals of higher social strata.[13] However, a different implication soon grew out of this rather sudden employment of self-enclosed rooms with a single door leading not to another room but to a corridor; the compartmentalization to keep an individual in a room resonated with the creed of the puritans' "'armoring' the self

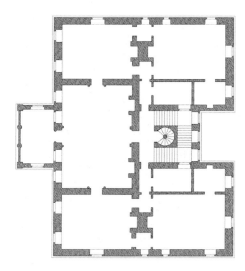

FIGURE 2.5 John Webb, Amesbury House, Wiltshire, 1661 (redrawn by Seho Kee based upon Robin Evans, *Translations from Drawing to Building*, Cambridge, MA: MIT Press, 1997, p. 73)

against a naughty world."[14] The solitude in a secluded room was to a degree a spiritual shield for the soul, detaching oneself from the interruption of seductive publicity and business. Evans wrote,

> With this came a recognizably modern definition of privacy, not as the answer to a perennial problem of "convenience," but quite possibly as a way of fostering a nascent psychology in which the self was, for the first time, felt to be not just at risk in the presence of others, but actually disfigured by them.[15]

This repugnance of the presence of or contact with others, along with seeking a confined sanctuary, prefigures the contemporary adherence to, or even obsession with, privacy. Passing the eighteenth and nineteenth centuries, "the corridor and the universal requirement of privacy" came to be finally set as the norm. Rooms were now distributed in such a way that each is equally nearby and remote. The room right next to this one and the room at the farthest are equally accessible through the thoroughfare spine, "a general strategy of compartmentalization on the one hand coupled with universal accessibility on the other."[16]

Evan's penetrating study into the historical formation of the central corridor and slotted rooms that suits the increasing stress on privacy is found to be instrumental in assessing the Japanese discourse on the corridor and shielded rooms. The Japanese intellectuals and the Europeans who criticized the Japanese house for its lack of a passageway were indeed caged within a historical moment in Europe; i.e., the nineteenth century in which the development of the corridor finally reached the status of a commonplace feature. Put differently, the shift in the history of Western architecture that occurred in Evan's portrayal somewhere between the sixteenth century and the early nineteenth century took place in Japan in a speedy manner during the late nineteenth century and the early twentieth century. In this development of the corridor, individualism and its correlate emphasis on privacy mattered more than class division—the initial cause for the formation of a corridor in Europe. The Meiji Restoration in 1868 officially dismantled the feudal and class systems, while providing the right to choose a living place of one's free will. The discourse to reform Japanese houses came at the turn of the twentieth century, about three decades after the Meiji Restoration. The discourse centered on Tokyo and on the port cities opened to Westerners where the effects of the dissolution of the class system were most strongly observed. What was conversely joined with the decomposition of the traditional feudal system was the increasing stress on individual rights in the context of the family and society. One representative figure who was vocal about these rights was Yukichi Fukuzawa (1835–1901). Influenced by his exposure to the political, economic and cultural systems of France and England, Fukuzawa repudiated the traditional feudal system. For him, along with the development of natural science, what made the West more advanced than East Asia was the idea of the equality of men. Independent individuals were crucial in constructing a new Japanese society in consonance with the materialistic transformation Japan was processing with the aid of Western technologies. In this context, Fukuzawa started the first chapter of *Recommending Learning* (*Kakumon no susume*) with a proclamation that,

> When the heaven gives birth to men, there is neither one above another, nor one below another . . . At the moment of birth, there is no distinction between the rich and the poor, and the noble and the lowborn. The only factor that makes distinctions among people is learning. One who has learned with efforts how the matters in the world operate becomes noble and rich. In contrast, the one who does not pour efforts to learning becomes base and poor.[17]

This emphasis on equality led him to redefine the family, too. The traditional Confucian hierarchy crowned by the husband was superseded by the union of two independent individuals of the same degree of economic, moral and social responsibilities. Hence, it was not coincidental that Fukuzawa was the founder of *Jijishinpou*, a newspaper where "How to reform the house (*kaokukairyoudan*)" was serially published.

The wall, fan and the wind conduit

Safeguarding privacy, eliminating noise, and ensuring functional clarity, the wall, or the interior fixed divider that separates one room from another, was accepted without reservation by architects of the 1920s and 1930s. This rather uncritical espousal of the Western norm defined creativity to be a mere matter of how the Japanese timber frame is combined with the Western stylistic image, or how an enhanced Japanese look on an interior constructed out of the balloon frame is engendered. For instance, Setsurou Yamamoto (1890–1944) experimented with how to formulate a Western stylistic exterior, while utilizing the Japanese construction method.[18] The Japanese timber frame was articulated on the exterior with a high-pitched roof, installed with vertically proportioned windows, and finished with wooden boards for the first story and stucco for the second story. Isoya Yoshida (1894–1974) presented another combinatory approach. While adopting the balloon frame, he revealed selectively timber structural elements to be contrasted with the otherwise column-free look of the Western method (Figure 2.6). The result, according to him, was an enhanced simplicity that reminds one of the eloquently plain interior of the Japanese tea room architecture.[19] It is evident that both Yamamoto and Yoshida failed to ruminate upon the environmental and cultural connotation of the demise of flexibility and openness of the Japanese domestic space. Their debates on the combination between the

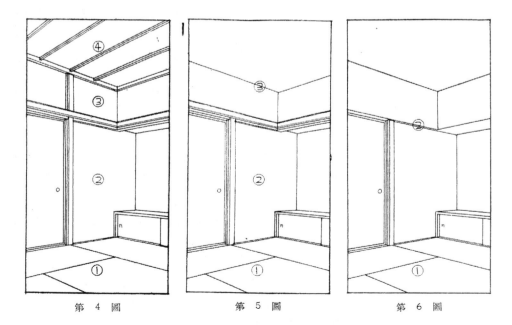

第 4 圖　　　　　　　第 5 圖　　　　　　　第 6 圖

FIGURE 2.6 Isoya Yoshida (1894–1974) (source: Isoya Yoshida, "*Kindaisukiyajuutaku to meirousei*," *Kenchiku to shakai*, vol. 18, n. 10, 1935, p. 68)

Japanese structure and Western style and on the adoption of the Western structure with the effect of enhanced visual aesthetics was naïve; its implication on the relationship between the occupants and the climatic phenomena, and on the correlate transformation of the human relationship was not envisaged.

Despite the benefits fixed interior walls brought to the domestic space, such as the acquisition of privacy, it came with an environmental problem: minimized wind access and, more importantly, the disappearance of cross-ventilation throughout the house. There appeared a technological solution to this; what complemented the environmental discomfort of high temperature and humidity in secluded rooms was the electric fan. As a matter of fact, the electric fan had been imported in the early Meiji period and was one of the earliest electric appliances introduced from the West to the Japanese household. The electric fan soon became manufactured in the middle part of the 1890s by Shibaura Manufacturing Company (later renamed as Toshiba) and mass production began in 1916. The following four characteristics were settled as the features of the fan in Japan: black color, four blades, protective covers and head rotation. Curiously, unlike in the West where ceiling fans were popular, the Japanese favored fans that could be placed on the floor or on the desk. The reason came from the structure of the Japanese house, where the often flat and low ceiling was unsuitable for the installation of a fan. There was, however, another reason which relates to a climatic characteristic of Japan. The Japanese summer is hot and humid in contrast with most parts of America and Europe where summer is hot, but not as humid. For this combination of heat and humidity, the desk fan that offers a direct wind onto the skin to formulate the immediate effect of palpable cooling was found more suitable than the ceiling fan, whose effect is not instantly felt on the skin. This provision of direct wind became more necessary as fixed walls eliminated cross-ventilation. For this reason, while electricity was quite expensive for the lower levels of society, owning an electric fan became an object of desire among the Japanese across different walks of life and even operated as a symbol of social status.[20] At any rate, the fixed walls and the fan now became two inter-dependent components of a set in the history of housing planning in Japan.

In reference to this historical trajectory, one architect who merits much attention is Kouji Fujii (1888–1938). His approach was distinguishable from other architects in that he experimented with ventilation, while accepting both the functional division between rooms and the central corridor. Like Watsuji, Fujii was deeply interested in the *fudo* of Japan. Fujii's orientation was, however, different. Watsuji treated *fudo* not as the subject of natural science, but as the medium through which common subjectivity, or "who we are," is objectified to result in collective cultural measures and creations. In contrast, Fujii's approach was rather scientific. Comfort, dependent on such factors as humidity and temperature, was the key issue for him. Regretting the fact that there had been no previous study regarding the standard of comfortable temperature and humidity in Japan, Fujii referred to thermodynamic and metabolic research accomplished by Western scholars, in particular Leonard Hill (1866–1952) and Max Rubner (1854–1932). Fujii's conclusion was that 17.78 degrees Celsius was the ideal temperature, and 65 percent was the ideal humidity. He further analyzed the environmental performances of traditional Japanese and Western architecture in regard to temperature, humidity and ventilation. For him, the trend of accepting the *modus operandi* of Western houses was unsatisfactory, if not reckless, as it did not consider the environmental characteristics of Japan. The Western houses can be espoused, but only in such a way that they are customized to work favorably in Japan's climate, particularly in summer, which is hot and humid.

FIGURE 2.7 Kouji Fujii (1888–1938), exterior, *Chochikukyo* (1928) (photo by author)

FIGURE 2.8 Kouji Fujii (1888–1938), living room, *Chochikukyo* (1928) (photo by author)

Chochikukyo (1928) (Figures 2.7, 2.8), Fujii's fifth house, was the ultimate experimental work in which he concentrated all the devices and tactics for environmental management to stand the sweltering summer. The plan of the house centered on the living room, additionally positioning hall, dining room, kitchen, bedroom, and reception room (Figure 2.9).

FIGURE 2.9 Kouji Fujii (1888–1938), plan, *Chochikukyo* (1928) (redrawn by Dasoul Park based upon Kazuko Koizumi, *Nihonnojuttaku toiu jikken: fudo o 'design'shita Kouji Fujii*, Tokyo: Noubunkyou, 2008, p. 43)

The northwest corner of the living room was connected with a corridor that runs northward (Figure 2.10). The exterior was, in general, defined not by operable partitions but by walls and windows. Simultaneously, the layer that mediates between the inside and outside, such as an *engawa*, or the Japanese veranda, was minimized. One *engawa* was indeed placed on the south side, but was interiorized in consideration of winter coldness (Figure 2.11). Due to these features, the house was pretty much Western in its configuration, despite the fact that it had rooms of *tatami* mats along the central corridor. The qualities of the Western houses—removal of noise, functional divisions and privacy—were

FIGURE 2.10 Kouji Fujii (1888–1938), view to the corridor, *Chochikukyo* (1928) (photo by author)

FIGURE 2.11 Kouji Fujii (1888–1938), *Engawa* placed on the south, *Chochikukyo* (1928) (photo by author)

adequately accomplished. Despite its Western configuration, Fujii was environmentally alert. The buildable part of the land was oblong, having its long axis run from north to south. He situated the house along this axis, allowing the southern portion to benefit from its exposure to the sun in regard to heating and lighting. However, when it came to the issue of ventilation in the interior, the Western configuration of the house was found ill-prepared. In particular, the living room at the center, which should have the most ideal environmental atmosphere for its accommodation of collective activities, was isolated, not having any immediate exposure to the outside. The task given to Fujii was then to introduce wind into the interior with a central corridor and with a living room designated as its center.

Along with such devices as a ventilation opening on the ceiling and an opening on the floor to invite cool air into the interior from the crawl space (Figures 2.12, 2.13, 2.14), a curious device was a wind conduit. The site sloped downward along the west side, while remaining relatively flat or sloping upwards on the other sides. The slope on the west was thus found suitable for the placement of the mouth of a wind conduit (Figure 2.15). The conduit then traveled a rather long distance before it reached the living room, first under the ground, then through the crawl space below both the four-and-a-half-mat room and the three-mat room. Fujii set the level of the rooms about twelve inches higher than that of the living room so that the other mouth of the conduit would be exposed to the living room (Figure 2.16). In this fashion, he was able to bring wind to the depth of the living room, while not interfering with the privacy of the other rooms. If the house had been planned in the traditional manner, it goes without saying that the wind conduit would not have been necessary. The exterior wall, the interior wall between the four-and-a-half-mat room and the three-mat room, and lastly, the divider between the three-mat room and the living room could all have been opened and coordinated to facilitate cross-ventilation. In the case of Fujii's house, however, the perimeter of the house was mostly defined by the combination of solid wall and windows, replacing the traditional combination composed of the columns, on one hand, and on the other the

FIGURE 2.12 Kouji Fujii (1888–1938), ventilation opening on the ceiling, *Chochikukyo* (1928) (photo by author)

FIGURE 2.13 Kouji Fujii (1888–1938), opening on the floor, *Chochikukyo* (1928) (photo by author)

FIGURE 2.14 Kouji Fujii (1888–1938), ventilation opening to the crawl space, *Chochikukyo* (1928) (photo by author)

floor-to-ceiling partitions. In addition, the trajectory of the natural ventilation that joined the four-and-a-half-mat room, the three-mat room and the living room was blocked at its beginning point by a built-in closet. While the sliding doors between the rooms still existed and seemed to operate to a degree, the living room in their immediate vicinity indicates that they would be opened only reluctantly for the fear of privacy being violated. Despite its ingenuity, Fujii's wind conduit was a sort of last resort to cool down the living room and to remove humidity on a summer's day while not disturbing privacy.

FIGURE 2.15   Kouji Fujii (1888–1938), beginning mouth of the wind conduit, *Chochikukyo* (1928) (photo by author)

FIGURE 2.16   Kouji Fujii (1888–1938), ending mouth of the wind conduit, *Chochikukyo* (1928) (photo by author)

"Self-less openness" of Japanese vernacular housing

Regarding the value of the performance of Japanese domestic architecture, Watsuji had a different stance compared to these three architects. His view was aimed not at transforming traditional architecture in accordance with Western criteria, but at rediscovering and refreshing its significance from the perspective of climate and the ethics of the inter-personal. As argued previously, for Watsuji, there is no such thing as a pure individual. One is an individual as much as he or she is part of 'we.' Put differently, Watsuji's man was never a solitary individual, but an individual necessarily situated in the collectivity of 'we.' One is thus individualistic and social at the same time, and the two qualities are dialectically joined, one quality negating the other constantly. The family, a form of 'we,' is built upon various forms of relationships beyond that of the male and female—a husband in reference to a wife; a parent in reference to a child; and an elder in reference to a younger. These relationships are dynamic, dialectical and oppositional, yet bound to each other. According to Watsuji, in Europe, "modern . . . capitalism tries to see man as an individual; the family, too, is interpreted as a gathering of individuals to serve economic interests."[21] In Japan, however, the house is never a locus of a solitary occupancy, but a locus of a family, the operation of which is dependent on the acknowledgement of these sets of opposites. Furthermore, prior to being a place for a family to live together, the house (*ka* or *ie*) represents the continuity of the whole family from the ancestor to the progeny. The head of the house acquires the authority through the reputation that has been accumulated throughout past generations. The present family thus lives under this historical burden of keeping the house (*ka* or *ie*) in an honorable reputation. Watsuji thus wrote, "The 'house' thus evinces most starkly the fact that the family as a whole takes precedence over its individual members."[22]

This difference in the conception of the family and the house between Japan and Europe is reflected in their urban structures. Watsuji first talked about the spatial structure of a typical European residential building. Here he seems to have had in mind a flat with multiple units. The building comprises a staircase for vertical circulation, a central corridor on each floor for horizontal circulation, and finally individual housing units. Watsuji pointed out that the internal corridor of the building is an extension of the street outside. The corridor is the street, and the street, the corridor. Further intriguing is the fact that when one enters a unit, one is encountered with another corridor onto which the doors of the aligned rooms open. In other words, the street outside has extended itself into the inside of the unit. Each room in the unit "by one motion of the hand can be made into an independent and self-contained house."[23] If a person rents a room in a unit, a postman must go through the corridor of the building, and then the corridor of a housing unit before he or she knocks on the door to the room in order to deliver mail. The street, the internal corridor of the building and the internal corridor of the unit are all public, their openness ultimately being negated as one reaches a room that can be locked for private occupancy.

In contrast, in Japan, first of all, the flat is not a favored type of housing. If a place is called a house, it must retain the quality of an independent separate unity, rather than being conjoined with other houses. This preference for a detached house characterizes the urban sprawl in Japanese cities compared to their European counterparts. Japanese cities are spread out, being inefficient in many aspects: more drainage, roads, tram routes, electrical cables and wires, gas pipes and public facilities, and more human energy spent for commuting. The preference is also verified by a clear division between "the house as 'inside (*uchi*)' and the world beyond it as 'outside (*soto*).'"[24] Taking off shoes when one enters the house is probably the most well-known enactment and symbol of the division. With this distinction comes the association of the inside of the house "with purity, cleanliness, safety, and intimacy (inside the group as well as inside a physical space)," while the outside is associated with "impurity, dirt, danger, and strangeness."[25] In contrast with Europe, coffee shops and restaurants in the street are considered completely foreign, "in no sense the equivalent in purpose of the dining room or the living room within the house. The latter are private to a degree with not the slightest character of the public about them."[26]

Once one is inside the house, however, complete openness prevails. He or she experiences a dramatic fluidity between rooms. While separation from the street through wall fences is strong, "within, there is nothing of the nature of the independence of an individual room."[27] A room is connected with multiple rooms. Family members travel from one room to another (Figure 2.17). *Fusuma* and *shoji* are there, but they do not work as "an indication of a desire for antagonistic or protective separation of the kind expressed by the turning of a key in a lock; nor indeed do they possess the capabilities of becoming such."[28] The division is "a division within the unity of a mutual trust . . . not a sign of a desire for separation."[29] Partitions may indicate the existence of antagonism among the members. When they are slid, however, what arises is "a show of a completely [unbarriered] and selfless openness."[30] In this locus of "selfless openness" (Figure 2.18), corridors—the narrow passages that allow access to disjointed, private rooms—are minimized, as one room is directly connected to another. As a result, in the house there is no corridor, or if inevitable, a minimized corridor. Diagrammatically speaking, the Japanese house is a set of rooms forming a single large room, or a big room subdivided into smaller rooms with no corridor, rather than a set of rooms *and* a corridor. Watsuji further wrote,

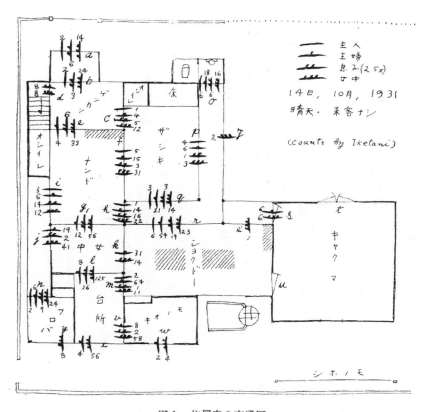

図 1　住居内の交通図

FIGURE 2.17 Plan of a vernacular town house and analysis of passages between rooms made by family composed of a husband (the straight line with no crosswise addition), a wife (the straight line with one crosswise addition), a son (the straight line with two crosswise additions) and a daughter (the straight line with three crosswise additions). (source: Kon Wajiro, *Kougengaku nyumon*, Tokyo: Chikumashobo, 1987, p. 329)

Fusuma and *shoji* have no power of resistance against anyone desiring to open them and their function as partitions, in a sense that is, always depends on the trust of others and their respect of the expression of the wish for separation indicated by the simple fact that they are drawn. In other words, within the "house," the Japanese feels neither need of protection against others nor any distinction between himself and others. A key indicates a desire for separation from the desires of others while *fusuma* and *shoji* show a unification of desires and are no more than a means of partitioning a room in this spirit of the absence of separation ... So the attraction lies in this tiny center of unity in the middle of the wide world.[31]

Watsuji's configuration predicated upon the ethics of the family confirms the primacy of the floor, ceiling, and partitions over the fixed wall and window. In this sense, his interpretation of the Japanese spatiality has something in common with, for instance, Bruno Taut's (1880–1938) view of the Japanese house as a stage, "an open-air theatre, the background of which, visible through the open wall, is nature.[32] Taut's characterization was correct and inspirational in the context of modernism, as it grasped the openness of the Japanese house where fixed walls are rarely found. However, Taut's interpretation did not consider the ethical background behind it, focusing more on the openness and its aesthetic relationship with the surrounding garden. What Watsuji instead revealed is the ethical, inter-personal basis that gave rise to the spatiality of the selfless openness.

Modernity and the duality between the inside and outside

Watsuji's discussion of barrier-free interiority in contrast with the outside acquires further significance on account of the Japanese experience of modernity. Watsuji wrote *Fudo* (hereafter

FIGURE 2.18 Openness of a Japanese house (photo by the author)

referred to by the title of its first English edition, *A Climate: A Philosophical Study*) at a historical moment in which Japan was undergoing a rapid process of modernization, a process that was initiated by the Meiji Restoration in 1868. The transformation was extensive, touching upon all aspects of society ranging from the political system, legal structure and educational structure to the metric system and fashion. Urban infrastructure was not an exception. Cars and trams were introduced. The roads had to be expanded and paved. Tram tracks were added. Electric street lights were installed, activating night life. The newly introduced train lines disrupted existing urban infrastructure, forming new commercial and entertaining sectors. Before he left for Germany, Watsuji considered the rapid changes in the cityscape caused by modernization to be normal (Figure 2.19). When he came back from Europe, however, he all of a sudden perceived the cityscape as very bizarre; in particular the relationship between transportation vehicles, such as trams and cars, and the houses. In Europe, means of transportation appeared "dwarfed" by the houses; they had a proportional harmony with the size of apartment buildings. In contrast, in Japan Watsuji found that they seemed oddly big; for example, a tram would block a house, so that the viewer on the opposite side of the street would only see the sky. Cars also seemed big in Japan, running like "a whale in a canal," and they seemed "both taller and somehow larger than a house."[33] These vehicles also seemed wild. To behold a tram running in the road made Watsuji feel as if he were "watching a wild boar rampaging through fields."[34] The wooden houses appeared powerless before the tram. Watsuji wrote,

> The tram is taller than the single storied house, longer than a house frontage and so stoutly built that if it were to run amuck, one has the impression that it would be the flimsy wooden houses that would be smashed into smithereens by its powerful onsurge.[35]

The same cars and trams appear completely different depending on where they are laid: in Europe, well-fit, and in Japan, ill-proportioned. For Watsuji, this absence of proportion between

Great Sight of Ginza.　　　　　新橋ノ上空ヨリ銀座ヲ瞰瞰セル銀座方面ノ偉観

FIGURE 2.19 Cityscape of Japan during modernization (Kjeld Duits Collection/MeijiShowa.com)

urban infrastructure and the house was a unique characteristic of Japanese modernity.[36] The turmoil of civilization was exposed "in such open, naked, candid and laughably strange terms."[37] For Watsuji, "the absence of balance thus discovered (a true condition of the urban scene in Japan) was already a part of what has been for a long time felt to be the tangle and disorder characterizing Japan's modern civilization."[38] The ethos of modernity in Japan consisted of this bizarre apposition between the Western urban infrastructure, where trams, cars and electrical street lights display their "primitively barbarous" charms, on one hand, and, on the other, the interiorized vernacular spatiality of subtlety and sophistication.

The juxtaposition also meant that the sense of separation between the house as inside (*uchi*) and the world beyond it as outside (*soto*) was deepened. The turmoil outside intensified the desire for separation. The outside roads where all forms of Westernization took place was boisterous, chaotic and restless, with beeping cars, honking trams and glaring neon signs. These machines were as primitive as they were advanced. The tendency of preparing a safe, secure dwelling place became stronger in the context of Europeanization and Americanization. As long as this turmoil was expressed in such roughness, crudity and primitivism,[39] Watsuji saw the role of the house with interiorized and sophisticated spatiality as growing more significant. He was confident that, despite the unavoidable process of social transformation, climate and its relationship with both the ethos of the Japanese and the spatiality of Japanese vernacular houses would survive.[40] That was because, in this type of house, he was convicted, "only [could they] relax."[41]

Joint measure and the spatiality of Japanese vernacular housing

Returning to the discussion of the openness of the interior in the Japanese house, this openness allows family members to formulate a measure *collectively* to a climatic phenomenon, such as humidity, heat, cold and so forth. In particular, this openness is efficient in responding to the Japanese heat combined with humidity in summer. How the Japanese house responds to the sweltering humidity has been a topic of study by many scholars. For instance, Noritake Kanazaki went through a meteorological analysis that compared the Japanese summer with other cities that were located between 30 degrees and 50 degrees latitude. The average humidity of Tokyo was 66 percent, hitting its peak in July with 77 percent and its nadir in May with 38 percent. These numbers do not seem to be striking, as they are low in comparison with the levels of the humidity of European cities—Rome (78 percent), Paris (79 percent), and London (84 percent). However, the level of humidity felt in Tokyo is higher than these numbers may indicate. In cities such as Rome, Paris and London, the months with high levels of humidity occur in winter, stretching from October to February. Accordingly, humidity is combined with low temperatures, and summers are therefore bearable. It is a different story in Tokyo. The months during which humidity is high are from June to September. During this period, the level of humidity is over 75 percent. What is combined with this humidity is heat. The temperature during this period is over 25 degrees Celsius. It is this combination of humidity and temperature that makes the Japanese summer unbearable. This phenomenon is not confined within Tokyo, as the whole country is mostly defined by an oceanic flow of hot air, with the exception being Hokkaido.[42]

Tokyo also has much rain. In terms of average yearly rainfall, Rome marks 735 mm; Paris, 614 mm; and London, 759 mm. In contrast, Tokyo marks 1460 mm. Again, this high amount of rainfall is a nation-wide phenomenon in Japan. The amount of rain Japan gets is almost equal to that of the tropical forests in Southeast Asia and South America. In the case of Japan, however, the rain is distributed throughout the year. Heavy and short-lasting showers like a squall are rare, except for the typhoon season in summer. This fact indicates that the Japanese climate is defined by heavy snow in winter, and hot and humid weather in summer, though there is a regional variation as the Pacific side receives rain more in summertime than in winter and the other side, more snow in wintertime.[43] The Japanese summer with high temperatures and much rain defines itself as part of the tropical or sub-tropical region, being influenced by monsoons, "a seasonal prevailing wind in the region of the Indian subcontinent and Southeast Asia, blowing from the southwest between May and September and bringing rain."[44]

According to Kanazaki, Japanese architecture responds to this climatic condition with various strategies. In response to the heavy rainfall and high level of humidity, it utilizes a wooden frame structure sitting on a raised platform. This approach is of course found unsuitable for winter coldness. However, what mattered more was not the walled protection against coldness, but how to cope with summer's heat and humidity, done by formulating ventilation—in particular, cross-ventilation. Indeed, in Japan, heating systems were less developed than in neighboring countries. For instance, Korea developed a floor heating system called *ondol* (Figure 2.20). The floor was constructed out of sheets of stones on top of which mud and oiled sheets of paper were applied. There was a chamber below the stones through which hot air, from the fire that cooks food in the kitchen, traveled and exited to a chimney positioned on the opposite side. In contrast with this distinctive heating system, the floor of the Japanese house was always built over a wooden frame. Heating was provided only locally by using portable devices such as *hibachi* (Figure 2.21) or *kotatsu*. To exaggerate, according to Kanazaki, the Japanese attitude about coldness is that it is fine as long as they can avoid getting frozen to death.[45] Of course, the Japanese perseverance over coldness indicates reversely the severity of humidity combined with heat during the summertime. The coldness of the Japanese house was thus an aspect often complained about by foreigners, as shown by Edward S. Morse's (1838–1925) grievance after living in Japanese houses, that, "the Japanese do not suffer from the cold as we do . . . Their indifference to cold is seen in the fact that in their winter-parties the rooms will often be entirely open to the garden, which may be glistening with a fresh snowfall."[46]

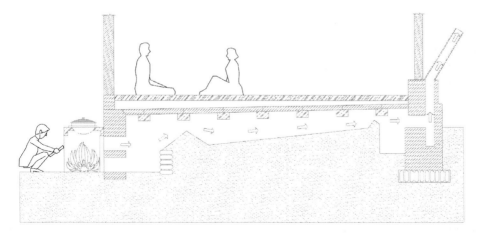

FIGURE 2.20 Korean floor heating system called *ondol* (drawn by Yi Liu)

FIGURE 2.21 *Hibachi*, a portable fire container (photo by author)

In architecture, along with the detachment of the house from the ground to cope with dampness, according to Kanazaki, materials were also chosen in consideration of their persever-ance against moisture. First of all, the hot and humid climate filled Japanese mountains with trees such as cypresses, cedars, pines and zelkovas, forming the well-known three beautiful forests: the cypress forest of Kisoji, the cedar forest of Akita, and the *hiba* of Aomori (*hiba* is a Japanese species of cypress). As Taut wrote, it is natural that the Greek built buildings with stones and the Japanese with trees.[47] In particular, the Japanese cypress endures contacts with moisture effectively, to the point that it can be built into a bathtub, counting itself, in particular its duramen, as the most valuable resource in wooden construction in Japan. Pines were used with *bengara*, or a ground hematite brought from Bengal, to avoid putrefaction. Chestnut trees were used for foundation for its resistance against moisture and decay. The Japanese cedar retains excellent capacity in absorbing and releasing moisture, and its oily nature resists decay. Its planks were used for the construction of walls and ceiling, and its small trunks were also used as the decorative column of the *tokonoma*.[48]

Compared to these features that are concerned with construction, materials and material treatments, however, Watsuji's discussion on the openness of the Japanese vernacular housing is unique. His discussion joins environmental benefits and the ethics of the inter-personal relation-ship. Indeed, the flexibility of the rooms has significance from the perspective of both climate and the expression of affection between the family members. On a hot summer's day, the flex-ibility between rooms allows a configuration in which partitions can be opened in such a way to facilitate cross-ventilation. A wind is invited from the street, through the screens (Figure 2.22), travelling through a room and continuing to flow into another room as the barrier between the two is lifted, until it reaches the small courtyard in the middle. Through this process, the wind has warmed up and carries humidity to be released to the atmosphere, an effective manner of removing heat and moisture without relying on machinery (Figures 2.23, 2.24). This configura-tion relies upon a *voluntary* sacrifice of privacy, a form of love existent between the family mem-bers. On a winter's day, the flexible spatiality also allows one to migrate effectively to the central part of the house where *irori* (a built-in fire), or *hibatch* (a portable vessel containing a few pieces of burning charcoal) emanates warmth. The family members sit around the source of warmth. The thermal tactility shared among the members of the household is one of the most of characteristic aspects of the Japanese vernacular architecture, as an author described:

> You have to have spent some cold winter evenings snuggled together around the *hibachi* (their portable little stove). Everybody sits together. A common quilt covers not only the *hibachi*, but everyone's lap as well. It's when your hands touch and you feel the warmth of their bodies—and everyone feels together—that is the real Japan.[49]

In this fashion, Watsuji renewed the significance of flexibility from the perspective of both climate and the expression of affection between the family members. As is commonly known, modernism framed the flexibility of Japanese architecture from the perspective of functionality and economy. Modernism also praised its spatial quality defined by a diagonal visual experience, as operable partitions between rooms can be opened in such a way that a straightforward axiality is avoided. What is missing in this rather functionalistic and aesthetic interpretation of the flexibility of Japanese architecture, however, is its environmental performance premised on a different dynamics of the human relationship in which the contemporary sense of privacy is not a guiding principle.

It is this aspect of a balanced sharing of a given resource, such as warmth in contrast with coldness and coolness in contrast with warmth, that characterizes Watusji's role of climate in

FIGURE 2.22 Front view of a *machiya* with various screens (photo by author)

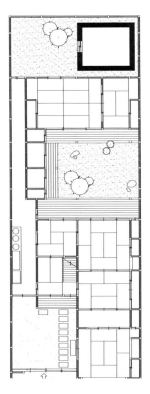

FIGURE 2.23 Plan of *machiya* (drawn by Hamed Aali)

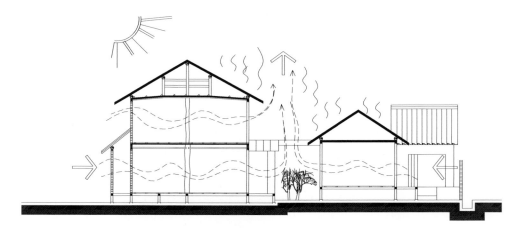

FIGURE 2.24 Analysis of cross-ventilation in a Japanese vernacular town house (drawn by Hamed Aali)

fostering the inter-personal. The shared warmth of a room on a winter's day by a group of people is coalesced with the warmth that defines the inter-personal relationship between the participants. As argued previously, warmth is *both* a physical quality and a quality of the inter-personal. The same holds true for other qualities such as coldness. In this regard, Watsuji's discussion of climate with the spatial arrangement of the vernacular Japanese house is a paradigmatic image of the social dimension of ecology—ecology regards not only the relationship of man to available resources, but also the relationship between man and man. Consequently, for Watsuji, at the basis of ecology is the inter-personal sharing of 'we,' in which scarcity itself is the medium of a proportionate joining.

To be sure, the meaning of "voluntary" in the statement above merits special attention. It should not be understood as echoing the tradition of egoism in which "voluntary" would be understood as the heroic act of ego's denial of its own self. When we are discussing Watsuji's *fudo*, we are standing on a different ground—the tradition of 'we' and no-ego. We should remind ourselves of the notion of '*ex-sistere*'—that the self-apprehension in a climatic phenomenon is not destined towards seeing the subject himself or herself. One becomes the 'I' among many 'I's imbued with the same climatic atmosphere. There is no such a thing as an isolated solitary individual before a pervasive climatic phenomenon; one is joined with another. The surplus of that which fills up the interiority of the self necessarily leads him or her to orient towards the outside world to search for that with which he or she can compensate the surplus. This self-transcending discovery is the basis for movement, creation and production. Watsuji wrote,

> In these experiences we do not look towards "the subject." We stiffen, or we put on warm clothes, or we draw near the brazier when we feel cold. Or, we may feel more concern about putting clothes on our children or seeing that the old are near the brazier. We work hard to have money to buy more clothes and charcoal. Charcoal burners make charcoal in the mountains, and textile factories produce clothing materials . . . In the same way, when we rejoice in the cherry blossoms, we do not look to the subject; rather it is the blossoms that take our attention and we invite our friends to go blossom-viewing, or drink and dance with them under the trees.[50]

The sufficiency of the self is overturned. What is revealed here is the fundamental openness of the self towards the world, or the fundamental orientation towards what stands beyond the I. This is the condition for the formation of what Watsuji called a "joint measure," as Watsuji wrote,

> The same may be said of the summer heat or disasters such as storms and floods. It is in our relationship with the tyranny of nature that we first come to engage ourselves *in joint measures* to secure early protection from such tyranny. The apprehension of the self in climate is revealed as the discovery of such measures; it is not the recognition of the subject.[51]

This joint measure is accumulated. It is not transitory, having historicity. It is not only the phenomenon of today, but also of the past, as other people also defended themselves in solidarity and the method they adopted has been succeeded to the subsequent generations. In other words, self-apprehension is accumulated over time to foster typicality in our relationship with climatic phenomena, operating as the basis for the formation of styles, customs, norms and habits. In this regard, the house is the self. More precisely, it is the collective self, the crystallization of the self-apprehensions of the members not only of the family but also of the group who live under the same *fudo*.

From collectivity to privacy

Despite the fact that Watsuji was convinced of the survival of the flexible spatial layout that embodied collectivity,[52] it became a convention during the post-war period to design houses based on what Watsuji would see as the Western conception of privacy. Indeed, the term "privacy" has a socio-cultural history in Japan. Before the process of modernization, in the traditional social relationship, there was no term that equaled the English word "privacy." The closest Japanese term would be "*uchi*," or inside defined by the boundary between a house and a street, or the boundary between a house and another, but not the boundary between a room and another. Put differently, "*uchi*" did not indicate the walls within a house that define individualized rooms. The word still meant the inside of the house as a whole, thus connoting the collectivity of the family, "a relationship admitting no discrimination."[53] In contrast, in contemporary Japanese, "*puraibashi*," or the Japanese pronunciation of "privacy," is now registered as a word. "*Puraibashi*" indicates the right of an individual not to be intruded upon or disturbed by anybody regarding a matter he or she sees as personal. Spatially speaking, "*puraibashi*" signifies the right of an individual to have a zone compartmentalized for a personal solitary retreat. This acceptance of the Western conception of "privacy" is attributed to a series of socio-cultural incidents. One would be the new Civil Code of 1947 that protected the rights of the individuals. The word also became popular through an incident in which a former foreign secretary "used the word [*puraibashi*] publicly to defend his personal life when he objected to the publication of a book detailing his divorce."[54] "Privacy" is now effective even within the relationship among the members of a family, defining a family as a group of equal individuals.

The spatial configuration of the typical contemporary housing in Japan now mostly follows what Watsuji would consider the spatiality of Western residential architecture (Figures 2.25, 2.26). Striking is the fact that the house is now typically divided into separate rooms that can be locked. In contemporary houses, concrete walls or walls of a wooden balloon frame replace the partitions. With this transformation, the potential of forming a larger whole for sustainable benefits is irrecoverably lost. Each room is environmentally controlled, nullifying any necessity to form an ensemble with another room by negating privacy in an unforced manner. What made this spatiality possible is air-conditioning. If the housing with fixed interior and exterior walls in Japan during the pre-war period was mechanically ameliorated by electric fans, as discussed earlier, the housing with fixed interior and exterior walls during the post-war period cannot be explained without discussing the development of air-conditioning. A room air-conditioner manufactured by General Electric (GE) was first imported to Japan by Shibaura (later renamed Toshiba) in 1935. However, due to its high price, its spread was limited and staggered compared to the distribution of the more affordable, though still expensive, fans. In 1952, the EW-50, the first room air-conditioner manufactured by a Japanese company, was released. This model was also called a "cooler," indicating its single function to cool down. Lacking a division between an indoor unit and an outdoor unit, it was directly installed on a window. Later in 1961, a wall-mounted type was devised by Toshiba. Splitting the system into an indoor unit (CLU-71) and an outdoor unit (CLA-7H), this model resolved the noise problem of the window model, as well as saving the window for viewing purpose. The role of the window was now fixed as more or less pictorial, as there was no need to open it to invite a fresh wind from the outside to cool down the room and to remove humidity. Even

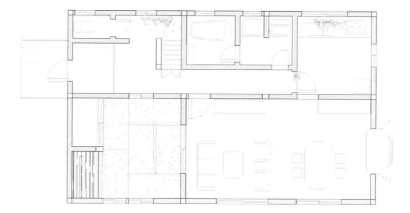

FIGURE 2.25   First floor of a typical contemporary house plan (redrawn by Rohan Haksar based on Ozaki, Ritsuko and John Rees Lewis, "Boundaries and the Meaning of Social Space: Study of Japanese House Plans," *Environmental and Planning D: Society and Space*, 24 (2006): 98)

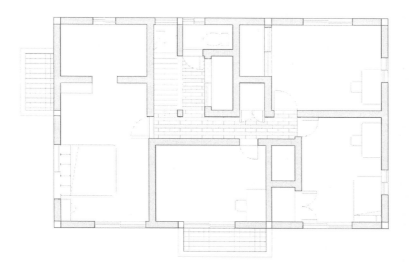

FIGURE 2.26   Second floor of a typical contemporary house plan (redrawn by Rohan Haksar based on Ozaki, Ritsuko and John Rees Lewis, "Boundaries and the Meaning of Social Space: Study of Japanese House Plans," *Environmental and Planning D: Society and Space*, 24 (2006): 98)

if wind had been admitted, its trajectory would have been greatly compromised. It would not be able to travel to an adjacent room to implement its efficacy and be released to the atmosphere, as rooms were walled off from each other. In this type of spatial configuration one would enjoy privacy, or the freedom to be secluded in a separate room furnished with a wall-mounted air-conditioner.

In the traditional house, particularly the category of the row house (*machiya* or *nagaya*), the boundary between the house and the street was articulated through various forms of screens. Rooms of the house were defined by operable partitions set within a timber framework, the floor and the roof operating as more permanent spatial definers. The boundaries between rooms were temporal, with the expectation of maneuvering the screens on the front and the partitions to invite a much appreciated cross-ventilation on a hot summer's day, which would pass from one end of the house to a small garden inside (*tsuboniawa*). The partitions also enabled an occupant to migrate to a different room to stay near the shared source of warmth on a winter's night. To reiterate, for Watsuji, climate is more than a physical, environmental issue; it is the issue of the collective ethos of a group of people and of how their inter-personal relationships can be articulated. Accordingly, the emergence of environmentally-controlled compartmentalized rooms had an effect that undermined, if not annulled, various forms of the inter-personal at the level of the family, such as parenthood, filial duty, brotherhood and sisterhood.

Contemporary *fudo*-sensitive house

Despite the prevalence of privacy-valued houses in which *fudo* has been erased, it is still possible to discover cases in contemporary Japanese architecture that validate, at least to a degree, Watsuji's cultural climatology and its correlative ethics of collectivity. One example is the Azuma House (1976) in Osaka by Tadao Ando, the architect of the Himeji City Museum of Literature (1991), which was dedicated to Watsuji (Figures 2.27, 2.28). From the perspective of climate, what is most distinctive regarding the Azuma House is its courtyard (Figures 2.29, 2.30, 2.31, 2.32). Its intimate scale reminds one of *tsuboniwa*, or

FIGURE 2.27 Tadao Ando, exterior 1, Museum of Literature (1991), Himeji, Japan (courtesy of Tadao Ando Architect and Associates)

FIGURE 2.28   Tadao Ando, exterior 2, Museum of Literature (1991), Himeji, Japan (courtesy of Tadao Ando Architect and Associates)

the courtyard of the traditional Japanese row house. However, there seems to be a difference between the two. *Tsuboniwa* is quintessential for cross-ventilation in the humid hot summertime. While providing privacy for the inside of the house, various types of screens on the front of the house allow the wind to come in. The wind passes through the interconnected rooms and removes hot and humid air as it reaches the *tsuboniwa*. In contrast, the front of the Azuma house, composed of a monolithic concrete wall with a punctuated entrance door, marks a striking contrast with the front of the traditional house composed of the subtle balance between privacy and openness to invite a breeze in. For this reason, the amount of wind admitted is minimized, failing to reach the courtyard in the middle of the house. Ando's courtyard seems less efficient than its traditional counterpart in terms of cross-ventilation.

Despite this fact, the raison d'être for Ando's courtyard cannot be explained properly without considering Watsuji's conception of climate. First of all, the configuration lacks any thoroughfare corridor to which all the rooms are attached. Rather, it is a big room divided into three interconnected smaller rooms, one of which is an open courtyard. Furthermore, the location of the courtyard is enigmatic; it intervenes between two rooms—one room operating as a family area and the other accommodating the dining room, kitchen, and single bathroom. The two bedrooms on the second floor are also separated by the courtyard and joined through a bridge. This courtyard is thus a nuisance—imagine an occupant in one of the bedrooms answering the call of nature on a chilly winter's night. However, Ando defended

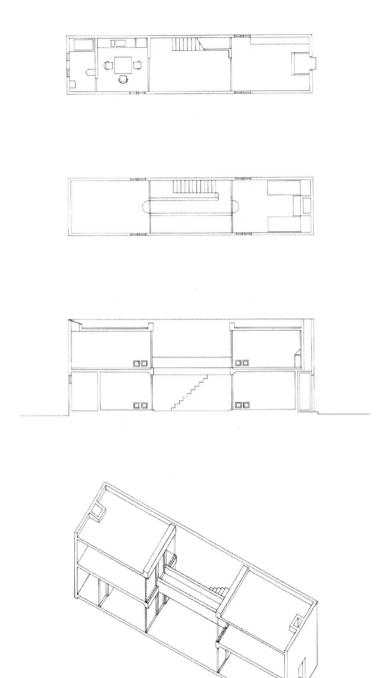

FIGURE 2.29 Tadao Ando, plan and axonometric, Azuma House (1976), Osaka, Japan (courtesy of Tadao Ando Architect and Associates)

FIGURE 2.30   Tadao Ando, exterior view from the street, Azuma House (1976), Osaka, Japan
(photo by Tadao Ando, courtesy of Tadao Ando Architect and Associates)

the courtyard as the place where one's relationship with natural things (*mono*) is renewed in the context of everyday life.[55] Like *tsuboniwa*, the courtyard is, in Ando's words, "a device to introduce the sense of nature composed of such elements as light, wind, and rainwater, things that are lost in contemporary urban life."[56] The restoration of the "relations between human beings and things (*mono*)" in the courtyard resuscitates the "sense of life" and the "feeling of substantial existence."[57]

Ando's use of the term "nature" merits special attention. As Ando clarified, the nature he meant is not a version of "pure nature" or "nature as such (*Ding an sich*)," a theoretical fabrication abstracted from the concrete experience of nature as it appears in our daily life. Rather, his interest was in the *relation* between human beings and natural things (*mono*). And, this relation was none other than "climate (*fūdo*)," the most concrete form in which nature *appears* in reference to human affairs. For instance, a rain that appears in the courtyard does not come as a collection of pure drops of water—like its molecular definition as dihydrogen monoxide. Rather, it comes as a form of rain imbued with human attributes, as well as seasonal and atmospheric qualities—*hakuu*, an elegant and sophisticated rain from a lucid summer sky; *ryudachi*, "a sharp summer evening shower"[58] after dark brought by heavy clouds (*ryudachikumo*) that cool down the earth; *samidare*, the tenacious and persistent downpours of the rainy season from June to early July; and *shūrin*, or the rain of autumn that accompanies melancholy.

FIGURE 2.31 Tadao Ando, view of the courtyard from the dinning area, Azuma House (1976), Osaka, Japan (photo by Tadao Ando, courtesy of Tadao Ando Architect and Associates)

FIGURE 2.32 Tadao Ando, view of the dinning area, Azuma House (1976), Osaka, Japan (photo by Tadao Ando, courtesy of Tadao Ando Architect and Associates)

In this fashion, the courtyard stages the rich variations of the Japanese climate under the formulas of, borrowing Watsuji's characterization, "the seasonal and the sudden" and of the combination between humidity and the sun that generates "a marked difference in the tone of the atmosphere."[59] Furthermore, as Watsuji argued, one's contact with these climatic phenomena is a matter not of objective science, but of keeping and cultivating the ethos of the Japanese— perseverance joined with fluctuating outflow, and sensitivity to subtle changes of mood combined with contemplative composure. Accordingly, for Ando, what makes the occupants of the Azuma House Japanese is the courtyard. What leads them to acquire the understanding of "who they are" is the shared courtyard that betrays the environmental comfort of conventional housing supplied by air-conditioned rooms chained through an efficient corridor. It is in this context that Ando claimed the courtyard as a place where the occupants acquire "the kind of self-knowledge that people today are losing."[60]

Notes

1 Seijou Uchida, Mitsuo Ookawa and Youetsu Hujiya, eds, *Kindainihonjuutakushi*, Tokyo, Japan: Kajima, 2008, pp. 36–7.
2 Terence Riley, *Un-Private House*, New York: Museum of Modern Art, 1999, pp. 10–11.
3 Ibid.
4 Ibid.
5 Robin Evans, *Translations from Drawing to Building*, Cambridge, MA: MIT Press, 1997, p. 59.
6 Ibid.
7 Ibid., p. 60.
8 Ibid., p. 64.
9 This type of configuration was indeed recommended during the early Renaissance, too. Evans quoted Leon Battista Alberti (1404–72) who, based on the practice of Roman architecture, wrote that "it is also convenient to place the doors in such a manner that they may lead to as many parts of the edifice as possible." Ibid., p. 63.
10 Ibid., p. 69.
11 What was recommended instead, for instance by Robert Kerr (1823–1904), was a room located at the end of an axis, a terminal room with only one deliberate door that could allow the occupant to control his or her connection with the remainder of the house. This shift from the convenience of having multiple doors in one room to that of having only one door preferably at a tactical point reflects an altered notion of domesticity in the West—from collectivity to the search of individual retreat. Ibid., p. 63.
12 Of course, the stairs and passages were present in the case of Villa Madama, too. However, they were less an independent passageway assuming the role of gathering and distributing traffic than a chamber being simply connected to another. Ibid., pp. 59–62.
13 The inception of the corridor was initially attributable to class division. Rooms on one side still had internal connections. However, parallel to the internal connections was a central passage running through the entire length of the house along which stand doors to rooms. A room can be directly accessed from the passageway without interrupting any other. Simultaneously, this device was efficient in controlling the movements of servants. Their presence in rooms such as a banquet hall was minimized, as they appeared to offer services and then disappeared immediately through the corridor. Ibid., p. 71.
14 Ibid., p. 74.
15 Ibid., p. 75.
16 Ibid., p. 78.
17 Yukichi Fukuzawa, *Kakumon no susume*, Tokyo: Iwanamishoten, 1942, pp. 11–12 (my translation).
18 The Western-style house utilizing the balloon framing was veneered to result in the disappearance of wooden vertical elements, or studs, on the interior. Along with the sliding sash windows, this column-free interior was considered a primary feature of the Western-style home. Yamamoto challenged this typical approach. Instead of repeating the conventional method of construction and its internal appearance, he adopted the Japanese method that articulates columns clearly, while filling the spaces in-between with fixed panels or sliding doors. He also replaced sliding sash

windows with sliding windows. An additional feature of Yamamoto's design included corridors effectively connecting different rooms including a living room equipped with a hearth, kitchen, dining room, bedrooms, library, and so forth. Rooms were designed to suit the sitting-on-the-chair style of living. Seijou Uchida, Mitsuo Ookawa and Youetsu Hujiya, eds, *Kindainihonjuutakushi*, Tokyo: Kajimashuppankai, p. 95.

19 Ibid., p. 99.
20 Hirano Kiyoshi and Ishimura Shinichi, "The Development of Electric Fan in Meiji and Taisho Early Days-Historic Analysis on a Design of Electric Fan (1)," *Bulletin of JSSD*, vol. 54, no. 3 (2007): 56.
21 Tetsuro Watsuji, *A Climate: A Philosophical Study*, trans. Geoffrey Bownas, Ministry of Education Printing Bureau, 1961, p. 144.
22 Ibid., p. 141.
23 Ibid., p. 162.
24 Ibid., p. 144.
25 Ritsuko Ozaki, "Boundaries and the Meaning of Social Space: Study of Japanese House Plans," *Environmental and Planning D: Society and Space*, vol. 24, 2006, p. 93; Joy Hendry, *Understanding Japanese Society*, London; New York: Routledge, 2003, pp. 47–8; Emiko Ohnuki-Tierney, *Illness and Culture in Contemporary Japan*, Cambridge: Cambridge University Press, 1984, pp. 21–31.
26 Tetsuro Watsuji, *A Climate: A Philosophical Study*, p. 164.
27 Ibid.
28 Ibid.
29 Ibid., p. 145.
30 Ibid.
31 Ibid., pp. 164–5.
32 Bruno Taut, *Houses and People of Japan*, Tokyo: Sanseido, 1937, p. 191.
33 Tetsuro Watsuji, *A Climate: A Philosophical Study*, p. 158.
34 Ibid.
35 Ibid.
36 Ibid., p. 161.
37 Ibid., p. 159.
38 Ibid.
39 Ibid., pp. 167–71.
40 Ibid., p. 202.
41 Ibid., p. 164.
42 Noritake Kanazaki, *Shikki no nihon bunka*, Tokyo: Nihonkeijaishinbunsha, 1992, pp. 8–12.
43 Ibid.
44 *Oxford Dictionary of English.*
45 Noritake Kanazaki, *Shikki no nihon bunka*, p. 19.
46 Edward S. Morse, *Japanese Homes and Their Surroundings*, New York: Dover Publications, 1961, p. 119.
47 Bruno Taut, *Fundamentals of Japanese Architecture*, Tokyo: Kokusai Bunka Shinkokai, 1936, p. 15.
48 Noritake Kanazaki, *Shikki no nihon bunka*, pp. 24–30.
49 Edward T. Hall, *The Hidden Dimension*, Garden City (New York: Doubleday and Company Inc.), p. 140.
50 Tetsuro Watsuji, *A Climate: A Philosophical Study*, pp. 5–6.
51 Ibid., p. 6.
52 Ibid., p. 202.
53 Ibid, p. 144.
54 Ritsuko Ozaki, "Boundaries and the Meaning of Social Space: Study of Japanese House Plans," p. 95.
55 Tadao Ando, "New Relations between the Space and the Person," *The Japan Architect* (November and December 1977): 44.
56 Tadao Ando, "*Sumiyoshi no nagaya kara kujo no machiya e* (From the Sumiyoshi House to the Townhouse at Kujo)," *Shinkenchiku*, 58 (July 1983): 173 (my translation).

57 Tadao Ando, "New Relations between the Space and the Person," p. 44.
58 Tetsuro Watsuji, *A Climate: A Philosophical Study*, p. 200.
59 Ibid., p. 199.
60 Ibid.

3

THE ECOLOGY OF 'WE' AND AMBIENT WARMTH

Richard Neutra's ecological architecture

Distanced from any romantic position of the natural such as that of Frank Lloyd Wright (1867–1959), Richard Neutra (1892–1970) saw the natural as imbalanced, if not imperfect. Human intervention is thus expected. This intervention is not for the sake of the anthropocentric and instrumental appropriation of nature and its resources, but rather intended for the restoration of balance between the different forces or qualities of the natural, articulating their right relationship peculiar to the character of a human abode. What is further important in reference to this human intervention is Neutra's sense of ecology. It is true that establishing the right relationship among natural conditions is an essential aspect of his ecological perspective. His sense of ecology, however, became further joined with the ethical dimension of the inter-personal that a human abode necessarily suggests. Indeed, the response to the natural and the dynamic of the inter-personal were not viewed as two different aspects, since the former operated as the agency that activated the latter. For Neutra, more fundamental than man's singular relationship with nature or natural resources was the inter-personal sharing of 'we,' in which scarcity itself becomes the medium of a proportionate joining. The coordination of a human relationship, such as a joint measure in coping with a natural condition, is a crucial factor that characterizes a setting to be ecological.

In further apprehending Neutra's notion of the environment and the correlate significance of human creation, his comment on the thermal quality of traditional Japanese architecture and its role in formulating the inter-personal encounter is essential. Neutra's interest in Japanese culture was undeniable. He often confessed his admiration of Japanese culture, he gave lectures in Japan in the 1930s and the early 1950s, and wrote about Japanese culture.[1] While these historiographical facts do add a degree of justification to this attempt to conjoin Neutra's architecture with Japanese philosophy, it is indeed in the theoretical connections that this section has more interest. Like Tetsuro Watsuji (1889–1960), Neutra apprehended a given context as consisting of invisible yet concrete forces. Creation for Neutra is concerned not with any imagery or code but with the coordination of the forces of *fudo*. In this regard, of particular interest is how Neutra established the relationship among fire, wind and water, and how he further conjoined this dialectical ensemble of the primary elements of cosmos with a daily setting for inter-personal activities. In particular, in underpinning Neutra's sense of the inter-personal communication in an atmosphere and the reciprocity between the natural and the inter-personal, this section adopts Watsuji's notion of an ego-less perceptual engagement with the surrounding and its trans-subjective communication of the 'we.' Watsuji's account of how one's relationship with the natural necessarily involves the dimension of the inter-personal is particularly significant for illuminating Neutra's practice, the goal of which was to secure a place for the inter-personal through the coordination of natural forces.

Beyond psychoanalysis and positivism

While focusing on the environmental lessons evident in Neutra's architecture in reference to Watsuji's philosophy, this section has two additional specific objectives. First, it seeks to uncover a new interpretive dimension that is latent in Neutra's architecture and goes beyond the currently dominant psychoanalytical mode of interpretation of his work. The psychoanalytical interpretation bases its arguments on Sigmund Freud's (1856–1939) characterization of the space-making as creating a substitute for the mother's womb and on the trauma of birth seen by Otto Rank (1884–1939), Freud's subversive pupil, as the etiology of anxiety in all other subsequent experiences of separation. House-making is thus apprehended as crafting a transference object to manage the trauma of birth and as accommodating the movement from the inside to the outside that reconfirms the original heroic will of the infant to become an entirely autonomous and independent being. The spatial continuity between the inside and outside Neutra embodied more dexterously than any other modern architect acquires a new significance. It is seen as nullifying the difference between the object-like character of the house and its spatial continuity with the outside infinity. The free-plan, a tenet of modernism, which smoothens and invalidates the traditional distinction between space and object, is considered "as a therapeutic technique, rather than as a creed of form and space."[2]

While acknowledging the validity of this kind of interpretation to a certain degree, it is equally true that Neutra distanced himself from the psychoanalytical tradition, in particular its ego-based delineation of the 'I,' thereby opening theoretical room for a quite different mode of interpretation. Rejecting the ego-based modeling of the human being, this section instead introduces a philosophical tradition of ego-less-ness and joins it with both Neutra's writings and his practice. In addition, instead of seeing the post-birth life as confirming the masculine autonomy of an ego-possessed infant in the space of continuity or the tenet of modernism,[3] this section views it as initiating the dimension of the inter-personal in various formats such as the filial, parental, friendly, erotic, pedagogical and so forth to move beyond that of the merely instinctual and physical. It then becomes very natural that, while psychoanalysis viewed the development of the vertical posture after birth and the consequent exposure of the genital area as initiating covering,[4] Neutra comprehended this development—an enactment of "facing"—as a form of engagement with the other, i.e., an emblem for 'we.' The philosophy of ego-less-ness also allows us to understand Neutra's dissatisfaction with any ego-based mode of communication such as empathy. It is also now clear that Watsuji's philosophy operates as the backbone when formulating an interpretation of Neutra's architecture, being distinguishable from its psychoanalytic counterpart.

The other objective of this section is to generate a more nuanced version of environmental ethics than the current positivistic approach taken towards the ecological crisis. It is true that to avoid any further environmental deterioration, discovering and utilizing new energy resources, in particular, renewable elements such as light, wind, rainwater and others, is urgent. What is indivisibly coupled with this framing of the natural elements is the advertising of innovative technological gadgets to be installed in a setting such as solar shading, intelligent facade, and photovoltaic panels. Here, the environmental crisis functions merely as another opportunity to globally reformat the building industry steered by high-tech corporations. The uniqueness of this opportunity consists in the fact that while it contributes to the cause of energy conservation, it simultaneously secures economic proficiency. In contrast with this positivistic approach, this section seeks to develop an ecological framework that offers room to the social and communal dimension as mediated precisely through man's relationship with the natural. In this framework, the reciprocity between the natural and the inter-personal, in which the former reinforces the latter, is the key to an ecological setting.

Coordinated balance of different forces

Neutra often wrote of Japanese culture. One good example is the foreword he wrote for *Japanese Gardens for Today* by David H. Engel (1959). In this writing, Neutra characterized the Japanese garden as retaining "the multi-sensorial appeal" of "the sounds, odors, and colors" and "the thermal variations of shade, sunlight, and air movements."[5] Undoubtedly, Neutra's observation of the characteristics of the Japanese garden reminds one of Watsuji's comments on the nuanced nature of Japanese *fudo*. By contrasting the Japanese climate with European counterparts, Watsuji sought to explain the nature of the Japanese art. In England and Germany, according to Watsuji, a foggy day is succeeded by another. In Italy and Greece, a clear day is the norm. This monotony of the European climates—some may find this characterization of European climates by Watsuji simplistic—led Watsuji to be awakened to the varieties of climatic conditions in Japan: "the cool of a summer's evening, for example, the freshness of the morning, the violent change, sufficient to bring cold at the sunset of an autumn day, the morning cold in winter, enough to shrivel the skin, and, after it, the balmy warmth of an Indian summer's day."[6] As discussed in an earlier chapter, an important point Wastuji strived to make was to prove the sophisticated nature of Japanese culture in response to Wilhelm Dilthey's (1833–1911) characterization that saw oriental art as primitively vital and semi-barbarous.[7]

However, there is another point with which Watsuji characterized the Japanese garden. Neutra did not talk about it, but understood its principle and applied it to his architectural design. Commenting on the characteristics of garden design between Japan and Europe, Watsuji employed as the lens the relationship between the natural and the artificial. In Greece and Italy, trees such as cypress and pine grow vertical perfectly even without the gardener's intervention. Order seems to be intrinsic to nature there.[8] In contrast, the sense of order in the Japanese garden is different. The principle of the Japanese garden emerges in response to the characteristics of *fudo* of Japan where "nature left alone is indeed disorderly and desolate confusion"[9] on account of the heat combined with humidity, the primary feature of a monsoon area that turns forests into jungles especially in summer. A type of art cultivated in Japan was accordingly distinguishable from that of the Greeks who did not feel any "urge to elevate" their love of a natural beauty, as observed in theatres, into "idealization."[10] It was also distinctive from the culture of the Romans who developed art that was "entirely artificial and geometrically precise."[11] The garden of the Este Villa at Tivoli serves as a good example characterized by the "carving up of soil or plants by geometrical straight lines or by circular paths."[12] Watsuji argued, however, that this kind of garden marks itself less as an idealization of the beauty of nature than as its artificialization. In contrast, the art of Japan takes a different path that acknowledges mutuality between the natural and the artificial to realize idealization of the order latent in nature. Formulae such as "making the artificial follow the natural"[13] and "nursing of the natural by the artificial"[14] guide the designers of the Japanese garden. Watsuji wrote,

In the matter of grasses, for example, if those that obstruct and those that serve no purpose are removed, nature then reveals her own order. Thus the Japanese discovered a purely natural form within the disorder and wildness of nature and this is what is reproduced in their garden. In this sense, the Japanese garden is indeed a refinement and an idealization of natural beauty.[15]

Watsuji qualified further what the order to be shaped through "nursing of the natural by the artificial" was like. What was revealed through the removal of what is unnecessary was reciprocity of a unique kind between different elements of nature. The shape, tactility and arrangement of elements were defined not by any geometrical rule, as in the Roman example, but in their mutual relationship to formulate an ensemble of non-geometrical and trans-formal harmony. The artificial intervention to tend nature meant to give life to an element by formulating a contrasted balance, a form of mutually enlivening reciprocity, between the element and the others. Wastuji wrote,

> In the case of an austere garden, there may be nothing other than a single pine growing from a flat surface of moss or five or seven paving stones . . . There is no diversity to be unified here so that it could be described in essence as nothing more than a simple unity. The moss, however, does not grow naturally over the whole surface thus. It is artificial in that it has been achieved by tending. What is more, the moss does not form a simple plane cover on the surface of the kind that would be given by turf cut and trimmed. The gentle green of the moss has an undulation that wells subtly from below. This undulation belongs to nature, untouched by man; yet man, realizing the true beauty of this subtle natural undulation, has given it life by his tending of the natural. So the garden builder gives close attention to the relationship between this soft undulating green and the hard stones. The way of cutting the stones, their shape, their arrangement, and even whether the surface be plain or whether the shape be square are all determined from considerations not of the achievement of a symmetrical and geometrical unity, but of a contrast with the soft undulations of the moss . . . Here is a unity gained not by geometrical proportion but by a balancing of forces which appeals to the emotions, a unity of a meeting of spirit . . . Every effort is made to avoid the orderly in order to achieve this "meeting of spirit."[16]

The artist of a Japanese garden positions things in such a way that their qualities create a coordinated balance. What was desired through "the connection of balance, this meeting of spirit"[17] was life, not a static aesthetic quality but a matter of spirit in which one is there because of the presence of its opposite. Consequently, the garden embodies not an academic symmetry that follows a geometrical disposition and regulation, but a harmony of contrasted forces, a higher level of symmetry. Here it is worth reminding one of the scene Watsuji looked upon as distinctive of the monsoon: "The bamboo, a native of the tropics, covered in snow."[18] This combination of a woody plant of "a tropical belt" and ice crystals of "a frigid zone"[19] is none other than a balanced coordination of two contrasted forces: heat and cold. The strikingly contrasted balance between opposites—an encounter between the green leaves and branches, on one hand, and, on the other, the white crystals that accentuate its life on account of the lifeless background of a plain snow-covered winter field—is the order of nature to be artificially fostered, operating as the guiding principle for a creative act.

Anchorage and the coordination of forces

Neutra was probably not aware of Watusji's literature that interpreted the principle of the Japanese garden as consisting in the coordination of different, even opposing, forces. However, this does not mean that he was unaware of the principle itself in his architectural practice. Indeed, one of his primary architectural principles was the very coordination of forces. In order to understand his sense of order as balancing of different forces and the correlate task of architectural creation, I'd like to explore first, anchoring or how to situate a building on a land, in Neutra's architecture. Neutra often emphasized the significance of anchoring a house in a site. He saw anchoring a shelter in a spot as the act of securing a resting place for soul. Neutra wrote:

> Home, I could muse in another mood, is soul anchorage, a psychosomatic mooring place, which higher organized life, from coral colonies to rooted horsetails and pine trees, and finally, to man, seem somehow to tend to. And, really, tumble weeds, migrating fish to spawn here, migrating birds to breed there, are anything but homeless or geographically indifferent. Quite the contrary, they are the most sensitive to the spot.[20]

To a degree, Neutra's strategy to realize the anchorage of architecture was similar to that of Wright. Like Wright, Neutra's residential architecture relied for the sense of anchorage on the presence of the fireplace. Neutra was also inspired by Wright's treatment of corners. By opening up corners in such works as the Kaufmann House (1935), Wright devised a dialectic between centrality characterized by the fireplace, which is surrounded by cave-like, rough course masonry, and the periphery defined by the openness of the glassed-corner towards nature outside. In a sense, Wright's space had two visual foci complementary to each other. The space was not about the mono-directionality of either from the inside to the outside, or vice-versa. Rather, it embodied a co-presence between the centripetal and the centrifugal. Neutra was indeed fascinated by this treatment of corner with glass by Wright, which provided "visual openness" and "protection against air movements that are prone to be particularly strong at a corner of a building."[21] This interest in corner further reflected his observation that "in the free landscape or on restricted sites, surrounding circumstances very often invite a more or less diagonal relationship of a building and openness at a corner."[22] Following and developing Wright's treatment of corner further, Neutra was able to achieve a concordance between interior and exterior in a dramatic fashion. He wrote:

> Sometimes fascinating affinities can be developed between interiors and outside spaces which are lying directly "in front" of them but in slanted directions. Sometimes such diagonal outlooks are of the greatest charm and significance. They may even lie directly and diagonally opposite to entrances to interior rooms or to areas within them which are dedicated to outlook. It may be the bed of a sleeping room which has such an outlook when the rising sun changes the color of clouds over the water area, a lake, the sea; or it may be just an interestingly shaped or blooming tree which becomes a soul refreshing feature by making a corner transparent.[23]

The Miller House (1937) in Palm Springs, California, is one example among many in which one can witness the co-presence between the centrality of the fireplace and the peripheral openness of the corner. Neutra places a fireplace at the center of the front wall in the living room and simultaneously he opens up its southeast corner to introduce both morning sunlight and the view to the distant horizon (Figures 3.1, 3.2). Neutra then placed a raised daybed at the corner, relating it both to the fireplace and the openness of the corner. The daybed was the spot where one could experience mutuality and co-existence between the two poles: centralized interiority characterized by the fireplace and peripheral exteriority defined by the horizon. This collage was analogues to the dynamic composition accomplished by an artist like Pablo Picasso (1881–1973), who "endeavored to give the brain dynamic composition of what one visually experiences from opposite sides."[24]

However, Neutra's interest went beyond the visual joining of what is near and what is far and was conjoined with the concern to augment activities of dwelling. In the case of the Miller House, the corner was granted an extended roof (Figure 3.3). Of course, this additional covering enhances one's visual experience from the inside towards the outside, as it frames the view to the desert. However, it was also a device contributive to the augmentation of the practices of dwelling inside, as it formulates a shade on the periphery of the house where the corner and the daybed are located. The space below the extended roof was occupied by a lap pool, a device which, in conjunction with the ceiling inside, reflects and softens the otherwise intense quality of light before it is introduced to the interior. To the south of the corner was a screened porch extending the inside dwelling activities to the outside. Lastly, the design of the window at the corner itself deserves to be commented upon

FIGURE 3.1   Richard Neutra, Miller House, view from the living room, 1936 (© J. Paul Getty Trust. Used with permission. Julius Shulman Photography Archive. Research Library at the Getty Research Institute 2004. R. 10)

FIGURE 3.2 Richard Neutra, Miller House, view from the living room through the screened porch to the southeast, 1936 (© J. Paul Getty Trust. Used with permission. Julius Shulman Photography Archive. Research Library at the Getty Research Institute 2004. R. 10)

in this regard (Figure 3.2). It was divided into two sections: bottom and top. The bottom section is composed of one single pane of fixed glass. In contrast, the top section is further composed of three vertically-proportioned units, among which the two closest to the corner are operable. This window—an ensemble of two different sections—assumes different roles: filtering through the bottom section a direct wind for the occupant who stays on the day-bed, and simultaneously admitting wind indirectly through the upper section. The former conforms to what Neutra defined as violent winds, which, according to him, "have been recognized by tests as troublesome to conceptual numerical brain operations."[25] A couple of benefits emerge from the latter. First, it introduces wind in a refreshing manner, like a breeze, which functions as the carrier of non-visual qualities of the outside environment such as smell, humidity, and sound. Second, the fireplace benefits from this introduction of wind which carries oxygen. Of course, the fireplace is tangentially positioned from the axis along which the wind flows in (Figure 3.4). However, this is precisely what Neutra envisioned for the relationship between fire and wind. Through devising a tangential encounter between two, Neutra avoids a situation in which the fire grows uncontrollably, and seeks to leave fire suitable for the dwelling activities of the occupants.

In this regard, the daybed was the place where one could sense the coordinated mutuality of forces such as fire, water, wind, and light. And, they encountered and interacted with

FIGURE 3.3   Richard Neutra, Miller House, view from the outside to the corner and screened porch, 1936 (© J. Paul Getty Trust. Used with permission. Julius Shulman Photography Archive. Research Library at the Getty Research Institute 2004. R. 10)

each other in an agreeable manner. This point clarifies the difference of Neutra's anchorage from that of Wright. Neutra's anchorage was not only about the hearth. Nor was it confined within the issue of creating a cubism-like dynamic visual composition in which the far and the near reciprocate in concordance. Rather, Neutra's sense of anchorage lay in the formulation of balance among the primary elements of cosmos and their forces. This balanced and harmonious encounter guaranteed the place to be a peaceful resting spot for the human soul. To a certain degree, what the proportional balance of different qualities, or the juxtaposition and interaction of fire, wind and water presents, is a formula, like "the fire set between wind and water," bringing about two contrasting moments of potentiality: first, the fire going wild for the wind with its abundant provision of air and, second, the fire going to extinction for the water with its unlimited power of bringing things down. Accordingly, the formula opens a spectrum between the flame's constant vertical mobility and the flame's calming down to turn flat in accordance with the platform. In particular, with the latter, the deep calmness of the ashes, or the death of the fire in horizontal stillness, approaches the ideal flatness of the platform and that of the reflecting pool. As much as the bed in a strategic location interacts with the fire deftly set between wind and water, its performance emerges in accordance with the spectrum between vibrant life and calm peace, a spectrum established by the sensorial and postural matrix of the fire. This spectrum does not exact a static choice of unfailing certainty, since neither life nor death is a choice, but a given. In contrast, the spectrum awakens in the perceiver the primary Gestalt of human experience conditioned by life and death, the two insurmountable ultimate opposites of the human living.

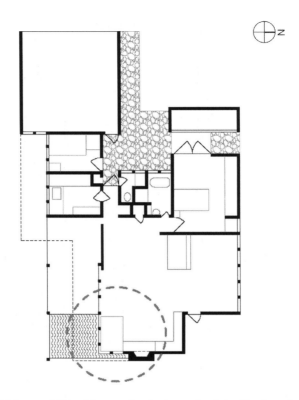

FIGURE 3.4 Richard Neutra, Miller House, plan (redrawn by Seho Kee based upon Arthur Drexler and Thomas S. Hines, *The Architecture of Richard Neutra: From International Style to California Modernism,* New York: Museum of Modern Art, 1984, p. 72)

The bed discovered in this spectrum is now the place of potentialities between, for instance, its role as the place for a burning desire of an erotic love and its role as the place of death with the promise of absolute peace. According to Neutra, a foghorn blowing its two base notes "[produces] an acoustical 'Gestalt' [. . .] over the irregular noise chaos of sea and forest."[26] The two base notes, "these lawful audible shapes are an anchorage for the consciousness and guidance through the uncertain and the bewildering, [. . .] appeasing the soul in the changing weather and turmoil of life."[27] Likewise, the presence of the fire set between wind and water in the Miller House resonates the two base notes of human living, life and death, in order to appease the soul in the turmoil of human survival driven by the competition of egos.

Illumination

I would like to point out one other decisive difference between Neutra and Wright in their practice of anchoring architecture to a spot. The Miller House was built on desert land to which nothing can be anchored. The house was based on a prefabricated timber frame structure, which was "a variant of the typical American balloon frame comprised evenly of spaced wood wall studs and roof joists."[28] Compared to Wright's Kaufmann House, in which the house was literally fastened into the depth of boulders and rubble masonry was exposed in its many parts, the Miller House was rather, according to Neutra, inserted, than anchored.[29]

In addition, except for the part structuring the fireplace, thick masonry walls were completely replaced by the layers of membranes sandwiching the wooden frame.

One effect of this disappearance of both anchoring and thick masonry wall is the loss of the sense of cave-like, enclosed protection (Figure 3.5). However, Neutra's frame construction addresses the issue of the sense of protection in its unique manner, eventually creating a kind of what I would call "open cave." In his own version of the story regarding the evolution of human culture, Neutra claimed that the discovery of fire as the source of warmth allowed man to come out of a cave.[30] With this anthropological development came the dramatic experience of openness demarcated by the distant horizon, a novel experience for the primitive man who had been residing in the confined and shady cave.

Then, one of the themes of Neutra's architecture was to augment openness and to comply with the memory of security provided by the thick wall of the cave, the emblem of protection. In this regard, I would like to bring one's attention to Neutra's treatment of light along the trough at the edge of the extended roof in the Miller House. Stephen Leet pointed out that this concealed lighting system was a measure taken to secure privacy at night in the house, a measure Neutra learned from the phenomenon that "plate glass acts as a mirror when washed with light."[31] Neutra thus succeeds in achieving to a certain degree rendering the windows, the emblem of openness, as walls, the emblem of enclosedness. For me, however, there is another dimension Neutra's lighting system accomplishes. For instance, at the rims of the ceiling in the screened porch—an extension of the living room which was often used as the studio for the Mensendieck system of exercise taught by Grace Lewis Miller, the hostess of the house—and of the roof above the lap pool was a continuous trough containing incandescent lights. At night, when it is lit, this porch and the space above the pool operate collectively as an additional thick layer of thermal device in which the ambient feeling of warmth spreads. Light, according to Neutra's anthropological story, was appreciated not only because of its brightness, but also because of its

FIGURE 3.5   Richard Neutra, Miller House under construction, November 1936 (courtesy of Jefferson and Philip Miller)

thermal value as the representation of warmth.[32] This symbolic value of light was further combined with the practical strategy to activate heat waves latent in light and to expand the edge of the house into a zone of warmth, as the smooth surfaces such as the polished concrete floor of the porch, panels of its ceiling, and the pool operate as reflecting devices. Imagine Miller who reclines on the raised bed at the corner. She feels the warmth emanating from the fireplace, simultaneously being surrounded at her back not by uneasy darkness, but by a layer of thick, softly illuminating warmth. This provision of a gentle, illumined warmth at the back testifies to Neutra's sensitivity to the physiological articulation of the lived body, which feels troubled and fearful when the unfathomable darkness of the desert and its coldness linger immediately behind the back. To have the feeling of being surrounded by thickened and luminous warmth and accordingly the sense of being protected is a precondition for the immersion of the lived body in a situation that may unfold in the heart of the living room. When Miller stands in front of a window, she does not face a fearful darkness storming her. Rather, the foreground has been salvaged from darkness to operate as the intermediary zone between the illuminated interior and the deep darkness. Neutra wrote:

> Seeing nights through living room windows or . . . experiencing an incredible widening of a room into the night landscape, which has its foreground salvaged from the darkness into photoscopic or color vision, are architectural measures and means entirely beyond the scope of the building art of the past.[33]

The compensation of the loss of thick wall and that of the sense of protection through the luminous warmth is more clearly observed in the Tremaine House (1947–48) (Figure 3.6) in Santa Barbara, California. In this house, Neutra designed a polished terrazzo terrace to expand the interior to the exterior, overcoming the picturesque operation of the windows standing between the two zones. The terrace was embedded with heating conduits, extending the warmth of the interior to the exterior and thus defining the exterior as if it were a part of the interior. Simultaneously, the terrace was combined with lights placed above on the soffit and lights placed outside at some distance away from the edge of the terrace. Because of the effective reflectivity of the polished terrazzo surface and of the ceiling, at night, the terrace comes to be filled with particles of light to stimulate heat waves of the light and to evoke the sense of warmth. Neutra wrote of this phenomenon occurring in the house with these words:

> The ceiling roof is a luminous lid, plastically modulated by illumination from concealed sources in upper and lower ceiling, lighter and darker strata that extend outward over the supporting framework. The polished Terrazzo floor forms a subdued reflection pool, underlying the structure, dematerializing its firm foundation and echoing, more faintly the play of light overhead. This becomes the major theme of the composition when the day is gone and night sinks.[34]

The dialectical operation between the luminous ceiling above and the polished terrace below envelops the periphery of the house with illuminated warmth. Surely, in the house, the heavy vertical wall of the traditional masonry construction is gone. So is the sense of protection emanating from the impregnable wall. However, such loss is deftly compensated by the thermal protection of the horizontally extended terrace. According to Neutra, the warmth extended from the interior to the exterior carries the "common memory" of the "even thermal offering" in the uterus, "a lovely sort of memory, an engram of . . . floating in warmth" into the life of

FIGURE 3.6 Richard Neutra, Tremaine House, 1947 (© J. Paul Getty Trust. Used with permission. Julius Shulman Photography Archive. Research Library at the Getty Research Institute 2004. R. 10)

post-birth.[35] While touching upon the common memory of the uterus, however, the provision of warmth were not aimed at a melancholic, solitary appeasement of the lost thermal memory of the uterus, either. Neutra wrote:

> In a way a house is the successor of the womb. But after leaving the womb, social interaction starts; the "post-womb shelter expert" shelters more than an individual, even if that individual is a bachelor—and he himself never works alone nor with his bare hands.[36]

For Neutra, the post-birth life initiated not the loss of the paradise, but the inter-personal discovery of "facing" the mother and the father, and other members of the family. Birth extends the physical and instinctual intimacy enveloping the fetus in the womb to different levels of the human relationship: filial, friendly, parental, pedagogical, erotic and so forth.

Warmth and the inter-personal in Japanese tradition

Continuing to discuss Neutra's sense of warmth, his remarks on the thermal quality of traditional Japanese architecture and its role in formulating the inter-personal encounter are essential. In a lecture delivered in Seattle in 1950, Neutra commented that "We are buffering off all the things which are unpleasant to the senses, and thus to the soul. Darkness by illumination, glare by shading, cold by heating, and heat by cooling."[37] In my view, what Neutra implied particularly in the latter part of this passage are two things. First, he was presenting a perspective in which the act of creation emerges as the act of restoring balance in an environment at the moment when its atmosphere is ill-proportioned for the excessive presence of natural qualities. Too much darkness as found in the night of nature is considered unpleasant to the senses and the soul; a balancing act to complement it through illumination is anticipated. Secondly, with this passage, Neutra also hints at the matrix between differences as a guiding principle in his architectural practice, like that of darkness and illumination in which the former is the condition for the presence of the latter. Here, the natural in excess, or in abundance if you like, operates as the agency for the formation and elucidation of the cultural. The sensitivity to this unique kind of continuity results not merely in a high-level, esoteric formal play. Rather, it gives rise to a setting in which contrasting atmospheres are gathered to correspond to the variegated spectrum of the human dwelling.

Warmth was particularly important for Neutra. Warmth implies the pre-presence of excessive coldness. One would compensate such coldness with warmth by firing wood or charcoal, bringing forces to an encounter and formulating an act of their coordination. This meeting of forces is most likely still imbalanced, as the coldness is excessive, for instance, on a chilling winter's night. It is precisely this moment in which a joint measure between human beings comes into being to cope with the still excessive coldness. Meeting of forces inspires the inter-personal joint measure to emerge as a quintessential resort. In a sense, the coordination of forces leads to, and is completed in, the coordination of the human relationship. It is in this context that Neutra was interested in the thermal behavior in Japanese culture, as it epitomized in this process of transcendence from the natural to the inter-personal. In a book review for Edward T. Hall's (1914–2009) *Hidden Dimension*, Neutra wrote:

> But he [Edward T. Hall] also understands in a flash an old Japanese priest who describes to him that you get to really know the Japanese on grounds of their thermal behaviors. "You have to have spent some cold winter evenings snuggled together around the *hibachi* (their portable little stove). Everybody sits together. A common quilt covers not only the *hibachi*, but everyone's lap as well. It's when your hands touch and you feel the warmth of their bodies—and everyone feels together—that is the real Japan." Whoever has been that intimate, as a foreigner! I had thought to have many wonderful friends in Japan, and felt, as an architect, very close to their homes, temples, gardens, taking them in through micro-detail, with almost all senses as does a Japanese. By some, the Japanese have been wrongly described as "voyeurs." I thought of them thus, judged from smell in their houses that they were olfactorially differently oriented than westerners, and as to their so closely lyrical, whispered recitation, or tender instrumental music in non-reverberant rooms, living in different auditive space.[38]

On a bone-chilling cold night, the *hibachi* in the Japanese household, a counterpart to the fireplace in a Western household, emanates warmth that penetrates the hearts of family members. The warmth is yet insufficient, occasioning a joint measure that conjoins the members into 'we.' The warmth of the bodies of the persons sitting tight is the reward of the joint measure to cope with the coldness that the *hibachi* alone could not compensate with. The circular configuration of the members around the *hibachi* emerges as a geometric idealization of the communal sense of 'we.'

Strikingly, Neutra's comment on the phenomenon of warmth taking place in a Japanese room is analogous to the way a climatic quality interacts with the perceiver as discussed in Watsuji's philosophy of *fudo*. As a matter of fact, Watsuji's philosophy operates as a theoretical reinforcement for Neutra's comments on thermal behavior. Watsuji claimed that, for instance, on a cold day in winter, coldness does not stand at the outside of the perceiver, but unfolds at the heart of him or her. From a diametrically opposite angle, claimed Watsuji, this means that the 'I' who is feeling cold is already out in the coldness. A thought that "I feel cold" in which the 'I' and the cold are treated as two separate entities emerges as an abstraction of this concrete experience in which the 'I,' a being of '*ex-sistere*' has already transcended its supposed boundary. The 'I' is not lost in this process of acknowledging the trans-individual background of the coldness. Rather, the shared coldness is precisely the ground for the articulation of a distinctive experience of the cold based on one's memory, character and capacity. It is in this context that in Japan the greeting in the morning is often characterized by the description of the weather itself: "It is cold this morning" or "it is hot this morning" is equivalent to the Western "good morning." One's discovery of the self—as in this case of the 'I' who is feeling cold—does not lead one to "look towards the 'subject [himself]'": the trans-subjective condition of coldness that is pervasive at the locale and has become particularized into the feeling of the cold in one's interiority leads him to "[put] clothes on [his] children" and "[buy] more clothes and charcoal."[39] By conjoining this subjective, individual awakening and the trans-subjective background from which it has emerged, *fudo*, or climate, operates as the basis for unconditioned compassion in interpersonal relationships, and for the formation of cultural measures.[40]

Returning to the Japanese household, it is the dimension of 'we' in the form of the shared, common warmth—this presupposes again shared coldness from which the act of creating the *hibachi* or the act of sitting closer to an existing *hibachi* emerged—that allows the members to feel each other, and, more importantly, to "face each other." In this facing is a deeper level of communication, as Neutra wrote:

> Communication . . . because you and I can look out of the same window and the same feelings come to us. We look at the dynamic flames and sparks in a fireplace beyond our noses—and what happens to you and me flows from one to another, the way music sounds in our parents' living room.[41]

Neutra often called empathy or "in-feeling" this shared phenomenon of warmth, in which each of the participants exists as an 'I' through its participation in 'we,' not a fragmented 'I' in separation from 'we.'

As a matter of fact, I believe Neutra's reliance on the term "empathy" to explain the common flow of an atmospheric quality such as warmth of the fire and sorrow of the minor-chorded melody to the hearts of occupants is not fully justifiable, if empathy is apprehended in its typical sense of the subject's capacity to project a quality from the side of his or her own self. While captured within the limit of the (Western) theory of empathy, in which the self is bypassed as full and sufficient and as the party which projects a feeling towards an outside phenomenon, what Neutra intended to explain was a deeper level of communication and sharing predicated on the potential of the self as pre-ego, emptiness, or capacity, to accept what is offered by the world. Of course, Neutra didn't mention this mode of the self that reminds one of Watsuji's theory of selfless perception. However, in discussing empathy, Neutra was certainly dissatisfied with the idea of the self as the retainer of self-sufficient and self-enclosed ego, a view which downgrades the self's sensational openness vis-à-vis the world. It is in this context that Neutra was critical of Freud's notion of ego and modified it into a new formula: the "sense-equipped ego." With this formula, Neutra challenged the non-bodily, self-enclosed condition of ego-centrism, the foothold in one's resisting the atmospheric flow originating from the world, and redefined it in a dialectic between enclosedness and connectedness, aloofness and openness, and interiority and exteriority. According to Neutra, the contribution of Albert Einstein's (1879–1955) theory of relativity is that it "introduced 'the observer,' the relativity of observation . . . , a sense-equipped *raisonneur*, into the detached drama of absolute space and time in Newton's universe."[42] Likewise, Neutra introduced a "sense-equipped ego" into the detached drama of the sense-less ego in Freud's psychology. Neutra's ego is open to the world through sensation and acquires the sense of the 'I' through this dynamic reciprocity with the world. As a matter of fact, I believe what Neutra was seeking to convey with this series of comments was the communicative mode of '*ex-sistere*' that transcends any mode of communication predicated on the conception of the 'I' as an *a priori* foothold. This mode of communication reinstates the condition of the human being as a pre-reflective corporeal being, or what I would like to call a "common subjectivity" to be articulated into different, yet conjoined, 'I's to form a collective body.

Facing and the ecology of 'we'

Lastly, I would like to reflect further on the issue of facing as the emblem of 'we.' In fact, Neutra singled out facing as the most significant postural articulation made by the lived body. He claimed rightly that in creating a posture in reference to a thing, one tends to turn towards it and face it. All things in front of us can be grabbed and embraced, while the things behind us cannot. Neutra wrote:

> Arms and hands, legs and feet are so jointed that the range of their effectiveness is greatest if we bring our body into a frontal relation to events in space. Our inner senses recording movement and posture tell us whether our body squarely faces an event to gain such effectiveness, be it facing a leaping lion or an approaching lover.[43]

This issue of facing was crucial in the context of the sacred space in Neutra's architecture.[44] However, it was also a matter of fundamental significance in the context of the domestic space, too. Neutra's interest in the promotion of collectivity between family members is clearly manifested in his positioning of, for instance, the dining table at the center of the house such as the Kaufmann House and the Tremaine House. Like the *hibachi*, around which family members gather, the table brings the members of a family around itself. It is true that, unlike the circular configuration formed by the *hibachi*, which embodies the ideal of equality, the table is still embedded with a hierarchical differentiation, as one of the two short sides or the middle point of any of the two long sides acquires the status of authority or attention. This point notwithstanding, the table functions as an emblem of togetherness, transforming the family into what Neutra called a "tight and dense community." Neutra wrote:

> One of the things which is recreational about tight and dense community is that you look into the faces of other people quite closely. I find this extremely refreshing to see a human face. When you are fender to fender as on that freeway, you don't get as much kick out of it as if you are face to face in that bus or elevator. I don't know whether you

can follow me on this, but there is something calming and exhilarating, in seeing human faces for an instant or two.[45]

Another moment that promotes facing in the context of the domestic space is accomplished through the diagonal openness of the glassed corner. As Neutra wrote in a previous quote, the openness at a corner, whose brightness is effectively contrasted with the surrounding darkness, attracts one's vision immediately when one enters a house. At this moment, one should note the fact that Neutra rendered the corner not only as a visual device, which leads one's vision towards a distant horizon, but also as the device of tight, but collective, occupancy, as was the case with the Miller House. The corner was thus a distinctive spot where the presence of other family members could be anticipated. In this way, the diagonal visual attraction of the corner is combined with the potential of facing between family members and their collective occupation. The corner now appears as a social and ethical device to formulate relationships between man and man, transcending its aesthetic role to join visually the interior with the exterior.

The issue of facing and the correlated collectivity of 'we' was not confined within the residential architecture, but operated as the grounding principle in Neutra's school architecture, too. Neutra's Corona School (1935) in Bell, Los Angeles, is a good example. The five classrooms were joined to create a linear block, and the south tip of the block was flanked by a wing (Figure 3.7). To the east of the block was a sheltered walkway and then a large, shared playground. In contrast, on the west side, each of the five classrooms was given what was called "the activity patio" demarcated by bushes. The boundary between a classroom and its patio was designed as a series of sliding steel doors laterally running along the track hidden in the ceiling. At a distance of some four feet from this layer of sliding doors was another layer of awnings operating vertically (Figure 3.8). The relationship between the horizontally operating sliding doors and the vertically operating awnings was constantly changing in reference to

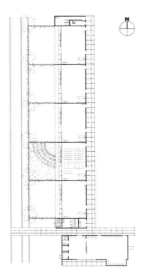

FIGURE 3.7 Richard Neutra, Corona School, site plan, Bell, Los Angeles, 1935 (redrawn by Myongjin Hwang based on a plan found in Architecture Archives, University of Pennsylvania)

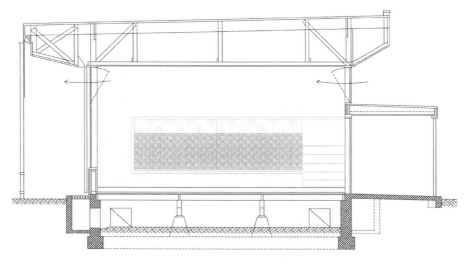

FIGURE 3.8 Richard Neutra, Corona School, classroom section, Bell, Los Angeles, 1935 (redrawn by Dasoul Park based on a section found in Architecture Archives, University of Pennsylvania)

the weather in order to secure a setting proper to the activity inside. While the sliding doors are wide open, the awning could be placed low to prevent glares from intruding the inside. When the sun is high, the awning could be lifted up completely, encouraging the migration of children to the outside. The boundary between the inside and the outside thus oscillates in reference to the trajectory of the sun: the shade of the classroom extends its grip onto the outdoor space on some occasions, and equally at other times the brightness of the outdoor space encroaches upon the shade of the classroom. The shaded cave of the inside is found at some times cold, and this shared coldness operates as the agency for children to conduct a measure by going out to the sunny patio in search of warmth. Conversely, on a hot day, the cool shade inside the cave-like classroom is found suitable, encouraging children to migrate from the outside to the inside. Unlike Wright, who, in his story of the anthropological origins of the human being and its related spatiality, favored the nomadic openness by criticizing the cave as the spatiality of non-democracy, Neutra joins the enclosed spatiality of the cave with the openness, adopting one for the augmentation of the other or as the giver of identity to the other.

The gathering at the "activity patio" in a non-hierarchical configuration of a circle—a format (Figure 3.9) that was often recommended by Neutra and was also implemented in other schools such as the Emerson Junior High School (1938) in Westwood, Los Angeles—replaces the conventional, one-directional facing between the teacher and the children in the classroom (Figure 3.10). Neutra at this moment accomplishes a version of the Japanese room in which everyone is "snuggled together" around the *hibachi*, facing each other. Seen altogether, the classroom and the patio form an ensemble between the cave and openness. Speaking in thermal terms, it is an ensemble between coldness and warmth, and coolness and hotness. It is also an ensemble of shade and bright openness. What is taking place in the students' transition from one zone to the other is analogous to the emphatic penetration of a thermal quality in the Japanese room. The warmth at the patio does not stay at the margin of the students' bodies, like a kind of stimulus to be checked by their mind or their inner subjectivity. It penetrates their depth and

FIGURE 3.9   Richard Neutra, model of the Ring Plan School, 1932 (© Cal Poly Pomona, College
of Environmental Design Archives – Special Collections)

imbues the depth with warmth. This sharing of the same warmth joins the students into 'we.'
(Again, this presupposes the students' sharing of coldness inside the classroom, defining them
into 'we' collectively in search of warmth.) The coolness of the classroom on a hot summer's
day is equally shared by the students and joins them into 'we.' Neutra married these communicative moments further with different types of mutuality: the one in the classroom is rather
formal and conventional, in which the one-directional relationship between the teacher and the
students is maintained, and the other in the patio, informal and spontaneous, promoting facing
existent not only between the teacher and the students, but also between students themselves
and thus redefining the teacher to be less an instructor than "a member of an active group."[46]
The migratory movements of children should not be seen as indicating their being unanchored
to a spot. In fact, their migration is attributable to their sensitivity to spots, confirming again
Neutra's words quoted previously, "migrating fish to spawn here, migrating birds to breed there,
are anything but homeless or geographically indifferent. Quite the contrary, they are the most
sensitive to the spot."

Put differently, for Neutra, continuity consisted in how a quality gives rise to another not in
similarity but in difference to form a dialectical ensemble. "Darkness by illumination, glare by
shading, cold by heating, and heat by cooling."[47] In my view, what Neutra implied particularly
in the latter part of this passage are two things. First, he was presenting a perspective in which
the act of creation emerges as the act of restoring balance in an environment at the moment
when its atmosphere is ill-proportioned for the excessive presence of natural qualities. Too
much darkness as found in the night of nature is considered unpleasant to the senses and the
soul; a balancing act to complement it through illumination is anticipated. Secondly, with this

FIGURE 3.10 Richard Neutra, Corona School, classroom setting, Bell, Los Angeles, 1935
(© J. Paul Getty Trust. Used with permission. Julius Shulman Photography Archive.
Research Library at the Getty Research Institute 2004. R. 10)

passage, Neutra also hints at the matrix between differences as a guiding principle in his architectural practice, like that of darkness and illumination in which the former is the condition
for the presence of the latter. Here, the natural in excess, or in abundance if you like, operates
as the agency for the formation and elucidation of the cultural. The sensitivity to this unique
kind of continuity results not merely in a high-level, esoteric formal play. Rather, it gives rise
to a setting in which contrasting atmospheres are gathered to correspond to the variegated
spectrum of the human dwelling.

Ecos and the inter-personal

Lastly, I would like to introduce a comment by Neutra, which he made before an audience
in Athens, that man does not live "in a vacuum, but in an ecology." In order to define what
he meant by ecology, Neutra introduced to the audience an etymological origin of ecology
and maintained that *ecos* meant the hearth, reminding one of Hestia, the Greek goddess of
domestic space. Curiously, Neutra then defined the hearth in the Greek residence as the
source "around which the balance of the family is found."[48] It is in this type of residence
that "one clinically meets 'him' and 'her' and their children."[49] This etymological study of

ecology was intended to point out the problem of contemporary housing. For Neutra, like ladies' hat business, architecture became a matter of business for changing tastes. This degradation of architecture was a partial reason for the dominance of "quick turn-over marriages and the high divorce rate."[50] While people worry about parking spots for their yearly changing models of cars, claimed Neutra, they have "no parking place . . . for their soul."[51]

Neutra's solution for this social problem was to design an ecological residence, like the ancient Greek residence with the hearth again as the source for the balanced relationship between family members. I think what is embodied in the Japanese room with a *hibachi* at the center reverberates to a degree the performance of the Greek residence. In the Japanese room, family members and their intimate guests sit together to share the same warmth emitted from the *hibachi*. It is this aspect of a balanced sharing of a given resource such as warmth in contrast with coldness, coolness in contrast with hotness, and shade in contrast with openness that characterizes Neutra's sense of ecology. Indivisible from this sense of ecology is Neutra's notion of continuity between the inside and the outside as the matter of a dialectical coupling of opposites, or the continuity of discontinuity. Neutra conceived the subject that conducts the act of restoring a proper proportional relationship between coldness and warmth, darkness and brightness, and enclosedness and openness not as the retainer of a detached mind, but as a bodily being with sensational capacity to pre-reflectively accept them. This bodily being is at the depth of the ego-self, being part of 'we,' as it is existent before the articulation of the 'I.' This type of subjectivity further clarifies Neutra's conception of the house not merely as a space of solitude represented by the melancholic, reclining posture of a bourgeois lady, but also as a domain of collectivity where the pre-reflective sharing of a resource with others in the zone takes place.

Referring to the cultural climatology of Watsuji, a climatic phenomenon such as coldness operates as the agency for the inter-personal. Thanks to the pervasive nature of *fudo*, or climate, the 'I' does not stand as an isolated or heroic independent entity. Rather, it is found in the middle of a climatic atmosphere such as coldness. What is further important is the fact that it is indeed not only the 'I' but also 'we' that is found in the middle of coldness. This condition—I would like to call it "common subjectivity"—is the basis for the articulation of different identities, their roles, and their actions proper to the distinctive roles. *Fudo* functions in this manner as the agency for the formation of mutual relations in which opposite roles such as father/mother, parent/child, and master/student are dialectically contrasted and inseparably joined. At this moment, one overcomes self-enclosed individualism to shape a collective cultural measure in conjunction with his or her opposites. This measure comes into being not because of empathy, which still presupposes the centrality of the 'I' as the active party that projects a feeling, but because of the mutually reciprocal bond between different 'I's as situated in the same atmosphere and as affected and embraced by it.

From this perspective, Neutra's architecture is a paradigmatic image of the social dimension of ecology: Ecology regards not only the relationship of man to available resources, but also the relationship between man and man, which Neutra idealized into the configuration of "facing." Consequently, at the basis of ecology for Neutra was not simply man's sustainable relationship with nature as a physical and objectified entity, which has been recently emphasized in the midst of the apocalyptic urgency to save resources. More fundamental than this positivistic attitude was the inter-personal sharing of 'we,' in which scarcity itself is the medium of a proportionate joining.

Notes

1 Neutra's appreciation of Japanese culture traces back to the period during which he was studying in Vienna, one of the European cities where *Japonisme* was in vogue during the late nineteenth and the early twentieth centuries. His further exposure to Japanese culture came into being with his apprenticeship in the Taliesin West where Wright often lectured on Japanese woodblock prints and culture. It was in fact through a Japanese colleague whom he met at the Taliesin West that Neutra came to be invited for two lectures in Japan in 1930, along the way to Brussels to represent America in the third meeting of the Congrès internationaux d'architecture moderne (CIAM). Neutra recollected that at the moment of arriving at the port of Yokohama he felt as if he were coming back home. Since this first visit, Neutra became deeply interested in Japanese architecture particularly in three aspects: the standardized process in the construction of dwelling spaces, while allowing individual variances; the integration between the architectural setting, on one hand, and the practice of dwelling and culture, on the other; and lastly, the significance of garden in terms of both enriching the quality of life of the occupant and activating the reciprocity between the inside and the outside. Neutra made additional visits to Japan in 1950 and 1951 to offer two more lectures under the titles of "To the fellow architects of Japan (*Nihon no kenchikukashokun ni*)" and "Return to nature (*shizen ni kaere*)." In these lectures, Neutra forsook the didactic attitude observed in the 1930 lectures under the titles of "The significance of new architecture (*shinkenchiku no igi to jitsusai*)" and "The international architecture ('*International' kenchiku*)." Instead, he confessed his admiration of Japanese architecture and acknowledged that Japanese architecture had been one of the primary beacons for his architectural design. Hiroyuki Tamada, "Richard Neutra's Architectural Thought and Japan ('*Richard Neutra' no kenchikukan to nihon*)," *Journal of Architectural Planning*, 2006, pp. 223–8.
2 Sylvia Lavin, "The Avant-Garde Is Not at Home," in R.E. Somol, ed., *Autonomy and Ideology: Positioning an Avant-Garde in America*, New York: Monacelli, pp. 185–9.
3 Ibid.
4 Sigmund Freud, *Civilization and Its Discontents*, trans. James Strachey, New York and London: W.W. Norton & Company, 1961, p. 54.
5 Richard Neutra, Foreword, in David H. Engel, *Japanese Gardens for Today*, Tokyo; Rutland, VT: C.E. Tuttle Co., 1959, p. xiii.
6 Tetsuro Watsuji, *A Climate: A Philosophical Study*, trans. Geoffrey Bownas, Ministry of Education Printing Bureau, 1961, p. 200.
7 Ibid., p. 171.
8 Ibid., p. 189.
9 Ibid., p. 190.
10 Ibid., p. 188.
11 Ibid.
12 Ibid., p. 189.
13 Ibid., p. 191.
14 Ibid.
15 Ibid.
16 Ibid., pp. 191–2.
17 Ibid., p. 193.
18 Ibid., p. 135.
19 Ibid., p. 134.
20 Richard Neutra, "World and Dwelling," UCLA Department of Special Collections Charles E. Young Research Library, Box 155, AAL-119, p. 2.
21 Richard Neutra, "Corners of Glass," UCLA Department of Special Collections Charles E. Young Research Library, AAL 121, paged as 362of.
22 Ibid.
23 Ibid.
24 Richard Neutra, "Reflecting Surfaces," UCLA Department of Special Collections Charles E. Young Research Library, AAL 121, paged as 362ah.
25 Richard Neutra, "Glass and the Wide Landscape Outside," UCLA Department of Special Collections Charles E. Young Research Library, AAL 121, paged as 362ah.
26 Richard Neutra, "Ideas," UCLA Department of Special Collections Charles E. Young Research Library, Box 193 (dated as April 7, 1954).
27 Ibid.

28 It was composed of "a combination of both typical two-by-four Douglas fir wood studs at 16″ on center and specially milled 2⅝″ by 3⅝″ wood posts at 3′ 2″ on center—a module set by the dimensions of Neutra's favorite steel casement windows, manufactured by Druwhit Metal Products." Stephen Leet, *Richard Neutra's Miller House*, New York: Princeton Architectural Press, 2004, pp. 95–6.

29 Richard Neutra, *Life and Human Habitat*, p. 238.

30 Richard Neutra, "Story of Habitation and the Home Design Today," UCLA Department of Special Collections Charles E. Young Research Library, Box 169, N-4, p. 1.

31 Stephen Leet, *Richard Neutra's Miller House*, p. 134.

32 Richard Neutra, "Story of Habitation and the Home Design Today," p. 2.

33 Richard Neutra, "Illumination and Glass," UCLA Department of Special Collections Charles E. Young Research Library, Box AAL 121, paged as 362ah.

34 Richard Neutra, "Illumination," UCLA Department of Special Collections Charles E. Young Research Library, Box 167, A-64 (AU-64), p. 1.

35 Richard Neutra, UCLA Department of Special Collections Charles E. Young Research Library, AAL-91, p. 10; Richard Neutra, UCLA Department of Special Collections Charles E. Young Research Library, Box 177, L-67, "Communication on World Issues Today," p. 2.

36 Richard Neutra, UCLA Department of Special Collections Charles E. Young Research Library, Box 159, A-116, p. 12.

37 Richard Neutra, "What Kind of a House Today?" UCLA Department of Special Collections Charles E. Young Research Library, Box 176, L-10, 1950, p. 3.

38 Richard Neutra, Book review for *Hidden Dimension* by Edward T. Hall (Reviewed for *Saturday Review*), May 1966, UCLA Department of Special Collections Charles E. Young Research Library, Box 175, B.R.2.

39 According to Watsuji, to claim that each has a distinctive sense of coldness is possible "only on the basis of our feeling the cold in common." Tetsuro Watsuji, *A Climate: A Philosophical Study*, Tokyo: Print Bureau, Japanese Government, 1961, pp. 4–5.

40 In this regard, I find Neutra's understanding of communication comes closer to the criticism of the theory of empathy presented by another Japanese thinker, Kitaro Nishida (1870–1945), the father of the Kyoto Philosophical School. For Nishida, the deepest form of empathy does not rely on one's capacity to project his or her own pre-retained feelings and emotions onto what is unfolding. On the contrary, it proceeds with the capacity to renounce those feelings and emotions and to transcend one's limit in order to formulate a complete unity, rather than any subjective framing, with what is unfolding. The unity Nishida had in mind was not static, but dynamic and creational. This is because the highest form of empathy is not at the moment of passive unity between the self-sufficient ego and the phenomenon, but at the very moment the ego is overturned for its limited capacity and starts to move toward the horizon of creation to accommodate the surplus. In the theory of empathy by Nishida is this higher form of unity, unity through creation. Such creation acquires the dimension of 'we,' as it is self-transcending, not self-imposing. Kitaro Nishida, *Art and Morality*, trans. David A. Dilworth and Valdo H. Viglielmo, Honolulu: The University of Hawaii Press, 1973, pp. 9–21.

41 Richard Neutra, "Communication on World Issues Today" (Notes on which Mr. Neutra based his address to the students of the Desert Sun School, Idyllwild, California), UCLA Department of Special Collections Charles E. Young Research Library, Box 177, L-67, p. 2.

42 Richard Neutra, "Ideas" (August 10, 1954), UCLA Department of Special Collections Charles E. Young Research Library, Box 193.

43 Richard Neutra, *Survival Through Design*, New York: Oxford University Press, 1954, p. 161.

44 Neutra's emphasis on facing also led him to appreciate the extension of the nave of St. Peter by Carlo Maderno (1556–1629). Unlike those architects such as Francesco Borromini (1559–1667) of the Baroque period and Le Corbusier (1887–1965) of the past century who criticized Maderno's extension, Neutra evaluated the extension from a different angle. For Neutra, the scheme by Michelangelo di Lodovico Buonarroti Simoni (1475–1564) was based on the non-directional, neutral, and omni-present spatiality that does not account for the physiological articulations of the lived body. Maderno's extension was positive as it gave directionality to the otherwise abstract and neutral space. This extended axis enables a pilgrim to approach the high altar step by step. This gradual forward movement towards the altar, a forward facing towards the holy was "an immortal part of all naturally founded ritual." The elongated axis monumentalizes the ultimate moment in which a believer stands in front of the Supreme Being. Neutra wrote:

> Wherever the Deity may be conceived to dwell, that ego, by its nature, would have to face it, prostrate itself before the supreme, use an actual and animated body in adoration, bend the head down in humility or raise eyes and hands upward in hope.

Richard Neutra, *Survival Through Design*, New York: Oxford University Press, 1954, pp. 161–3; For Le Corbusier's criticism of Maderno's extenson, see Le Corbusier, *Towards a New Architecture*, New York: Praeger, 1960, p. 171.
45 Richard Neutra, "Mr. Neutra's Free and Improvised Talk," May 9, 1961, Regent Lectures, University of California, UCLA Department of Special Collections Charles E. Young Research Library, Box 177, L-66, p. 24.
46 Richard Neutra, *Buildings and Projects*, Zurich: Editions Girsberger, 1950, p. 150.
47 Richard Neutra, "What Kind of a House Today?" p. 3.
48 Richard Neutra, Athens Lecture for Doxiadis Associates, UCLA Department of Special Collections Charles E. Young Research Library, Box 176, L-5, pp. 5–6.
49 Ibid.
50 Richard Neutra, "Mr. Neutra's Free and Improvised Talk," p. 21.
51 Ibid.

4

DIALECTICS BETWEEN THE REGIONAL AND THE TRANS-REGIONAL

In theorizing the inter-personal basis of sustainability, Watsuji's theory of *fudo* as intertwined with "who we are" is enlightening. Its elucidation of climate as pertaining to the dimension of the collective first opens a space for the reflection of the communal as circumscribed by a *fudo*. However, if his philosophy remains at the level of the collective characterized by the distinctiveness of the *fudo* of a region, it would share the same fate as any discourse on regionalism. The conservative insularity of the collective to the point of failing to acknowledge the presence of the others has been identified as the fundamental pitfall of regionalism. While it was not completely fledged, Watsuji's philosophy transcends the insularity of *fudo* and the communal to arise to the plane of the trans-*fudo* and the public. It is the plane where issues such as typicality of human praxis beyond regional boundaries surfaces, and its dialectical interaction with the idiosyncrasies of the region of which *fudo* is a vital part acquires significance. Watsuji's theory of *fudo* in this manner leads us to revisit Critical Regionalism, which sought to a degree reciprocity between the regional and the universal, or the trans-regional, a criticism of Critical Regionalism, and a discourse that deals with typicality of the ideals of the human living.

Fudo and beyond critical regionalism

In presenting six points of resistance to placelessness, Frampton prescribed as the fourth point a need to implement a public place where people encounter each other in an unforced manner (Figure 4.1). Here, he cited Hannah Arendt (1906–75), who believed "the only indispensible material factor in the generation of power is the living together of people."[1] On the other hand, Frampton criticized Robert Venturi for the reason that Venturi's architectural and urban position replicates the status quo of the American everyday life in which a room in a household with a television broadcasting sports replaces the public outdoor place such as a piazza. Curiously, in his discussion of the fifth and sixth points, Frampton prescribed a series of directions that embody the architecture of Critical Regionalism. Architecture of Critical Regionalism must make use of "local architectonic features against more universal and abstract ones."[2] It must also demonstrate sensitivity to local light, its range and quality, as well as to the topography of a given site. While the listing of these six points is significant in overcoming universal architecture without any character, however, there is a quandary from the perspective of Watsuji's philosophy of *fudo*. The problem in this omnibus-like display of six points lies in the fact that the connection between the fourth, on one hand, and the sixth, on the other, was never clearly articulated. Accordingly, making a place for people—the task of the fourth point—seems to be a task unrelated to the design of a building or a place that is sensitive to local climatic conditions, or the task of the sixth point.

There is a negative consequence stemming from this ambiguity. The disjuncture between the place of gathering among people and the place of climatic suitability can lead the prescription of the sixth point to be simply a celebration of sensorial richness. Indeed, Frampton's argument of vision and tactility leaves something to be desired. He criticized perspective for the reason that it is a "rationalized sight or clear seeing."[3] In a perspectival geometry, the lines and planes are parallel to each other converging to a point at infinity. Perspective presupposes an ideal spot where a perceiver can have a sweeping view of an urban scene. Every corner of the scene becomes clear instantly and transparently to the observer on the spot. As an alternative to the dominance of vision, Frampton recommended tactility. An example he cited was Alvar Alato's (1898–1976) Saynataslo Town Hall (1951) (Figures 4.2, 4.3). The hardness one may feel on the sole as he or she walks up the brick risers in the stairway leading to the main chamber is contrasted with the smoothness of the wooden floor inside the chamber. Frampton wrote, "The kinetic impetus of the body in climbing the stair is thus checked by the friction of the steps, which are 'read' soon after in contrast to the timber floor of the council chamber itself."[4]

While the criticism of perspective is valid and the recommendation of tactility is noteworthy, Frampton's discussion leaves something to be desired. Even though perspective operates in a rational, mathematical and focused manner, it does not mean that our vision inseparably

FIGURE 4.1 Urban piazza in Sienna, Italy (photo by Steve Cooke, courtesy of the photographer)

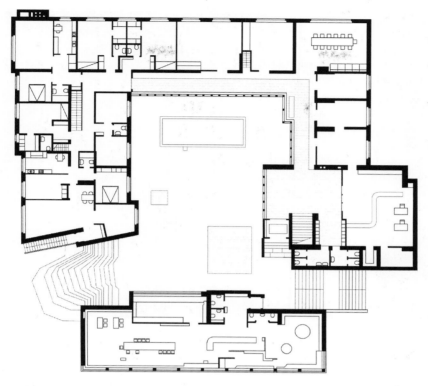

FIGURE 4.2   Alvar Aalto, plan, Saynataslo Town Hall (1951) (redrawn by Myongjin Hwang based on Richard Weston, *Alvar Aalto*, London: Phaidon, 1995, p. 137)

joined with the lived body operates in daily life in the same fashion. Listing just a couple of aspects of the everyday vision would prove this point immediately. The vision in the mundane is not able to screen all the things that fall within the scope of vision simultaneously and instantaneously, as if they were all assigned with an equal amount of significance. The world as perceived by the lived eye is indeed like a collage of intermittent scenes. The eye operates upon the dialectics between the silent and voluminous background, on one hand, and on the other hand, the figurative foregrounding. It also rests on the constant oscillation of the two—the background and the figurative foregrounding—in which a figure recedes into the background to make room for another emerging from the background. More crucially, Frampton's argument of tactility as a way of confronting a vision-dominated culture is embedded with the danger of celebrating tactility itself. What is not fully clear in Frampton's endorsement of tactility is the significance of a situation out of which a tactile experience would emerge. It is acknowledgeable that Frampton's tactility was situational, at least to a certain degree, as he justified the smoothness of the chamber in contrast with the roughness of the stairway from the perspective of establishing the chamber's "honorific status through sound, smell and texture."[5] On the other hand, Frampton's justification to overcome the dominance of vision also relied upon the sensorial seduction of a tactile quality with "its capacity to arouse the impulse to touch."[6] A simple question arises: Why does one touch, for instance, a concrete wall? Except in the case of one being an architect, professionally trained to examine and enjoy the tactile qualities of an architectural element, such as the wall in a frontal relationship, touching a wall

FIGURE 4.3 Alvar Aalto, courtyard, Saynataslo Town Hall (1951) (© Timothy Brown, source: flickr.com)

to appreciate its tactile quality per se occurs rarely in our daily life. A reason one may touch it is situational. The day is hot, and therefore a person looks for a shaded area and moves into the shade and leans against the wall. In other words, there is a pre-presence of a situation, or the world in the phenomenological sense, that leads one to touch the wall. Simultaneously, the touching is rarely frontal, but tangential: it is "leaning" and he or she feels the coldness on his or her back. If the pre-presence of a situation is not fully accredited, there is a danger of celebrating tactility itself, or the cult of tactility such as hardness, softness, shininess, glossiness, roughness, translucency, transparency, opacity, sleekness and so forth. An architect can display all the variety of tactile qualities of materials and elements; however, the issue hinges on whether the variety formulates an ensemble to uphold a situation in which the perceiver is involved, transcending a self-narcissistic aesthetic apperception.

Returning to the theory of *fudo*, what Watsuji's theory compensates for in the theory of Critical Regionalism is the interrelationship between sensation of climatic elements, and the situation of the inter-personal. In other words, Watsuji's theory offers a ground to join the fourth point and the sixth point, as listed in Frampton's Critical Regionalism. What is presupposed in the phenomenon of '*ex-sistere*', which defines "there" as the locus of different 'I's, is the body as the common medium, first of sensation, and second of action that emerges at the moment when the dimension of sensation is transcended. In this sense of the continuum from sensation to action, Watsuji's claim that reflection of the self through '*ex-sistere*' is not necessarily the highest mode of self-apprehension is noteworthy. In self-apprehension, according to Watsuji, our attention is not fixed on ourselves; one does not look merely at one's own self. Rather, one reaches out to the world. When one finds his or her self feeling cold, this moment of self-apprehension is not an end in itself. Instead, he or she comes to be necessarily connected with *acts*, such as looking for more clothes. Consequently, the discovery of one's own self does not confirm the insulated interiority of the subject. Rather, it reconfirms how one is interconnected with the world. Watsuji wrote, "In this self-apprehension we are directed to our free creation."[7] More importantly, in the phenomenon of self-apprehension in a milieu, the 'I' is joined with other 'I's, as Watsuji wrote that "it is in our relationship with the tyranny of nature that we first come to engage ourselves in joint measures to secure early protection from such tyranny."[8] Creations through the joining of different 'I's are the basis for what we call culture. Culture is thus "an inheritance of self-apprehension accumulated over the years since the time of our ancestors."[9]

Implied in the discussion of the '*ex-sistere*' by Watsuji is a tri-partite structure through which the body is embedded in the world and operates as the agency of its transformation. There is always a context or situation first, such as a hot summer's day. It is this climatic context that compels a father to face and move towards a shaded area, as the sensation of heat overflows the capacity of the body, which seeks to internalize the heat. The coolness of shade embraces the human body as if its coolness compensates for the overflowing sensation of heat to recover a balance, a kind of sensational balance. The father also invites the son into the same shade, as they were infected corporeally by the same heat. Understanding this mechanism, composed first of a pre-present climatic situation that is pervasive, second of common sensation, and lastly of communal and inter-personal action, is essential in justly mapping the strengths and weaknesses of the position that emphasizes sensational experience in architecture. It is in this mechanism that, for instance, the collective tuning of the partitions in Japanese vernacular houses to formulate natural ventilation for a communal benefit comes into being. Watsuji characterized the tuning as "selfless openness," in which the members of a family configure in one way or another the co-relationship among partitions of the rooms to make a thorough way for the trajectory of wind. Without understanding this tripartite structure from situation to sensation then to inter-personal action, emphasizing tactility can lead only to a cult of tactility. Tactility takes sensation as an end in itself, celebrating sensuous experiences and thus falling into the trap of aestheticism. I believe it is in this regard that Frampton's recommendation of tactility over vision offers only the first step we need to take into consideration when overcoming vision–dominant architecture.

While it has been a convention in architectural discourse to discuss sensation as if it were a matter of an individual,[10] what is more important is the sensation of all-together, or what I would like to call "common sensation," and most importantly the inter-personal act. Watsuji's discussion of the pervasive nature of climate that embraces different 'I's offers a theoretical background for common subjectivity beyond empathy. This common sensation that presupposes the shared corporeal datum of the human being is the basis upon which even individuals of different thoughts, values, backgrounds and customs initiate communication. In other words, the common sensation joins not only individuals of different 'I's, or the form of the communal where sameness prevails, but also *different* 'I's where differences are brought together through the mediation of the sameness. In phenomenological terms, if the relationship between one and coldness is that of intentionality, the relationship between different 'I's in the coldness is that of mutual compassion. The common sensational ground operates as the basis for compassion that is articulated in the form of parents inviting children on a hot summer's day into a shaded area. This compassion initiated by climatic phenomena functions as the basis for communication, such as greetings, conversation and speech, leading eventually to consensus and action. This social role of the shared corporeal datum is true not only in the typical versions of human relationships such as filial, friendly, pedagogical, erotic and so forth, but also unconventional ones such as an encounter with a stranger, or what is called "the other" in philosophical lingo, an encounter that is one of the most challenging moments in human relationships, as differences in terms of race, color, language, customs and so forth are brought together, exposed, articulated, negotiated, compromised and synthesized. The preferred format of this unmitigated encounter by Watsuji was the co-originating and co-dependent dialectic of opposites in which one is never self-sufficient, but is existent on account of one's difference with the other.

Fudo is the agency of the inter-personal relationship that is articulated through distinctive, yet mutually dependent, social identities. This aspect marks a culminating point in Watsuji's climatology. *Fudo*, or climate, is not just the environment between man and nature, but a social space we live in and share with, as Watsuji wrote in his study of ethics that the world of *fudo* is "not just the world of nature, but of . . . a society in which persons are related to each other."[11] Watsuji's extensive study of the significance of such Japanese characters as *ken* and *aida*, or such Japanese words as *seken* and *yononaka*, must be understood in this context of clarifying *fudo* as grounded in the inter-personal relationship. These characters and words speak of betweenness and are concerned with human relations, as well as the relationship between man and things. This inter-personal relation is not that of the relationship between an object and another, but, as Watsuji wrote,

> They are *act-connections* between person and person like *communication* or *association*, in which persons as subjects concern themselves with each other. We cannot sustain our-selves in any *aida* or *naka* without acting subjectively. At the same time, we cannot act without maintaining ourselves in some *aida* or *naka*. For this reason, *aida* or *naka* imply a living and dynamic betweenness, as a subjective interconnection of acts.[12]

Fudo as concerned with the relationship between man and natural phenomena is extended in its significance to be equated with a social space in which betweenness and "acting subjectively" are mutually reciprocating. How this model of the society by Watsuji predicated upon the mutuality of the two opposing dimensions is different from other versions of sociology goes beyond the scope of this work. From the perspective of architecture and urbanism, however, the inseparable bond of the two dimensions of *fudo* seems to have a lesson; it indicates that a social place without room for the intervention of climatic phenomena is to a degree flawed in its proper operation. A good example of the space where climate is deleted would be the prevalent shopping malls with air conditioning, where the inter-personal goes rarely beyond one seeing the other in a disengaged gaze of consumerism. An urban place characterized by *fudo* is conversely filled with the potential of fostering the inter-personal, as *fudo* is a pervasive phenomenon that has to be responded to in a collective fashion. Such a place is that of an event where speeches, actions and associations take place in the process of a collective tuning. It is also a place where differences are, as argued, brought together, exposed, articulated, negotiated, compromised and synthesized, precisely because of the shared pervasive climatic phenomena.

Criticism of regionalism

One noteworthy criticism of regionalism, if not directly of Critical Regionalism, was made by Alan Colquhoun (1921–2012). His criticism hinges around the political motivation of region-alism and its validity in the contemporary society. Colquhoun denounced a concern about region-based architecture sensitive to its climatic qualities as quite anachronistic. Colquhoun first traced the ideological origin of regionalism in reference to the nationalistic consciousness among European nations, some of which invented even fictional origins for their peoples and cultures. The motivation behind this political move was "the legitimization of a nation–state in terms of a regional culture."[13] Colquhoun considered regionalism as susceptible to conservative politics and even to its ultra-versions, such as the one that lays stress on racial purity. Regionalism in this case assumes an ideological role, being driven by a political situation in which a people or a nation faces a need to re-establish or even forge an identity for the consolidation and unity among its members. What was also connected with this search for a nation–state by mining the essence of a region was the conceptual distinction between *Zivilization* and *Kultur*. The former was oriented toward productivity and efficiency, and was thus materialistic, superficial and universal, while the latter was "instinctual, autochthonous, and particular."[14] This conceptual distinction granted validity to a degree to regionalism as it was considered a more authentic phase of history. For Colquhoun, "critical" meaning "resistance against the appropriation of a way of life and a bond of human relations by alien economic and power interests"[15] was then already part of the regionalist movements in Europe, consequently making this adjective in "Critical Regionalism" quite meaningless.

Furthermore, this regionalist concern is not only politically problematic for its origin and its susceptibility to conservative nationalism, but also for its out-datedness in reference to the *modus operandi* of the contemporary post-industrial world. While such concerns are of value to the third world, where different times—such as the agrarian and the industrial—co-exist, industrialized societies have different social agendas that "can any longer be expressed adequately in terms of the oppositions,"[16] such as *Zivilization* and *Kultur*. Regionalism simplifies the complex and already advanced picture of the world. Architectural and urban consequences of regionalism are unfortunate, too. Consciousness of the regional culture emerges precisely at a moment when a nostalgic attitude towards what has been lost surfaces. This condition defines architectural works of regionalism to be fundamentally a representation of what has already vanished. The works of regionalism thus fall down to the trap of composing formal vocabularies of the past, rather than being part of the continuity of history. A regionalist approach is secretively predicated upon what Colquhoun called the essentialist model—that a culture has a core filled with a specific set of codes, customs, folk songs and so forth. Discussing climate as one of the primary factors in formulating the architecture of regionalism also suffers from this essentialist model that reckons each society as "[containing] a core, or essence"[17] and is based upon a rigid and fixed relationship between cultural codes and regions. Colquhoun wrote,

> It is based on traditional system of communication in which climate, geography, craft traditions, and regions are absolutely determining. These determinants are rapidly disappearing and in large parts of the world no longer exist.[18]

However, in the contemporary society, "the regional differences are largely obliterated."[19] The correlation between cultural codes and geographical regions has evaporated. The codes are liberated from regions and appropriated in different locations. They become crotons of the equalized and instant mode of communication of the information age, which produces a type of difference in which flexibility prevails to form an unending series of differential plays in meaning by twisting, paraphrasing, replacing, substituting, joining and so forth. Colquhoun finally wrote,

> This, then, is the problem of architecture in the postmodern world. It seems no longer possible to envisage an architecture that has the stable, public meanings that it had when

it was connected with the soil and with the regions. How should we define the kinds of architecture that are taking its place?[20]

The one who conducts the play of mixing, shuffling and suturing assumes a hegemonic subject who knows which codes operate as the constituents of a national identity, who keeps himself or herself at a distance from the identity, and who makes an intentional play out of it to implement an intentional destruction of borders and boundaries. At the level of architecture, a figure enacting this insubordinate practice would be Arata Isozaki. Since his tangential involvement with metabolism, Isozaki presented a series of images of ruins, including Future City (1962), in which the ruins of Doric orders and the debris of metabolist structures were intermingled (Figure I.4). His Tsukuba Center (1983) commissioned by the National Housing and Urban Development Public Corporation is another example (Figures 4.4, 4.5). Isozaki betrayed the governmental expectation that the building should express a new Japanese identity as a major leader in technology by playfully combining vocabularies borrowed from the West, such as the piazza of Campidgolio by Michaelanzelo di Lodovico Buonarroti Simoni (1475–1564) and the columns at the portico of the House of the Director at the Royal Saltworks at Arc-et-Senans by Claude Nicolas Ledoux (1736–1806).

Fudo and the resuscitation of the corporeal efficacy of a code

Colquhoun's claims are convincing. They clarify the nature of the codes in the post-industrial society; that they are never fixed to a region, but float around to be selected, twisted and

FIGURE 4.4   Arata Isozaki, model view, Tsukuba Center (1983) (courtesy of Arata Isozaki and Associates)

FIGURE 4.5 Arata Isozaki, exterior, Tsukuba Center (1983) (photo by author)

manipulated as fragments, shards and debris. However, I believe it is still meaningful to ruminate upon the issue of the co-relationship between the code and the region, and the communicability of the code. In other words, the emphasis on the codes trespassing regional boundaries overshadows a couple of the possibilities of which Watsuji's *fudo* is indicative. The code acknowledged in the theory of *fudo* is the one that has recovered its sensorial and corporeal basis. A good example for the code that is not a merely informative sign to be easily manipulated beyond regional boundaries and that is equipped with a corporeal efficacy would be the cross in the Church of the Light (1989) by Tadao Ando (Figure 4.6). The cross as the universal symbol of Christianity refreshes its significance by joining itself with the light of the local area. In other words, the cross by Ando is qualitatively different from the type of the code that Colquhoun discusses, in that this cross joins both the universal and the regional as effectuated by its climatic conditions.

In illuminating the sensorial and corporeal significance of the cross, a discussion of the setting of the church itself is essential. The church is a simple concrete box with no insulation. In winter, being inside the church is still cold. What is important to understand is the fact that this coldness is not merely a physical phenomenon, but carries cultural significance. This coldness keeps the believers awake and leads their bodies to remain alert. It also keeps the believers from becoming overly ecstatic to the point that their conscious and rational commitment to Christ is disrespected. Indeed, this emphasis on the intellectual aspect of belief characterizes the Japanese Christianity as the religion of the literate compared to, for instance, Shintoism espoused by the public. In particular, the Non-Church Movement, an indigenous Christian society established by Uchimura Kanzo (1861–1930), put emphasis on the rational side of belief. It is in this context that one of his disciples, Gyoshin Kim (1901–45), recommended a cold shower even in wintertime in order for a Christian to keep his or her spirit awake. In consideration of this emphasis on rationality that was concretized through the thermal tactility of coldness, the intentionally cold environment of the Church of the Light functions as a space where a rational approach to Christianity takes place. The thermal quality of coldness that embraces one who has stepped into the church has a ritualistic dimension of him or her being showered with cold water. Dramatically, however, there is a reversal in the church. The light that is introduced into the church shines through the coldness, brightening and warming up the space, however slight it might be. It is the light of warmth whose efficacy is all the more enhanced for the pre-presence of the coldness, as well as darkness. The light is not just a physical entity, nor its warmth just a physical quality. Rather, it has a cultural significance, analogizing itself to Jesus, who himself was light emanating warmth. The coupling of coldness and warmth in the church is that of the rationality of the Japanese intellectual believers, on one hand, and, on the other, the irrational, unfathomable warmth of the divine love. The church operates as a setting where breathing cold air and feeling warmth are combined in such a way that augments spirituality.

What is also worth commenting on is Ando's original intention to leave the cross bare so that it operates as a wind channel.[21] As a matter of fact, the church as it stands leaves something to be desired in terms of ventilation. The floor-to-ceiling window on one side of the church is fixed and is blocked at a distance by a free standing wall. The slit on the rear wall is set with fixed glass. In terms of ventilation, the interior is quite hermetically sealed off. One could only imagine how hot the place could be during the particularly sultry Japanese summers. A situation observed in the Church in Tarumi (1993) (Figure 4.7), another Christian church by Ando that has similar conditions in terms of ventilation, illustrates what would happen during the summer in the Church of the Light. Fans are placed everywhere to alleviate the heat and offer relief through the provision of much-needed breeze during the service.

While the intention to leave the cross open was not carried out for fear of harming the health of the pastor, who would be directly influenced by the coldness in winter, it is regrettable that seasonal operability of the cross was not given due consideration in the process of design. Of course, operability would modify the appearance of the cross where glass is set with sealant to meet Ando's minimalistic intention. Allowing operability would require: reformatting the proportion and dimension of the cross; sub-dividing glass further for the setting of frames; and installing fixtures such as a handle. It is unclear whether Ando's inattentiveness to seasonal operability was due to another intention to secure an unprecedented degree of iconic clarity for the cross or the aesthetic tenet of minimalism.[22] However, neither of these reasons is entirely convincing: in the former, spirituality is not denigrated but enhanced at the moment when the iconic clarity engages with practical performance; and in the latter, primacy must be given to performance, not to aesthetics. One then asks: What would have happened if the cross had been made operable, rather than being finished with fixed glass or left bare? Had the cross and the backdoor been opened in a joint manner, a cross-ventilation would have surely emerged. What is characteristic of this ventilation is that its source is the cross, as if wind is the gift of Christ. Like the enhanced efficacy of light amidst the background of darkness and coldness, the efficacy of wind is heightened on account of the fact that it comes in as a thrust through a slit-like cross, rather than through a grand window. On the day of the Pentecost, the thrust of wind overlaps with the "rushing mighty wind,"[23] the former operating as a *palpable* metaphor of the latter. Is this cross merely another example of the code as discussed by Colquhoun? This cross is qualitatively different from the signifier, which is informative

FIGURE 4.6 Tadao Ando, interior view, Church of the Light (1989) (photo by Tadao Ando, courtesy of Tadao Ando Architect and Associates)

FIGURE 4.7 Tadao Ando, interior view, Church in Tarumi (1993) (photo by author)

and cerebral without any corporeal resonance with the perceiver, and which eventually develops into an empty one systematically emancipated from its referent. In other words, one's engagement with the cross does not yield a meaning of cerebral aridity, but acquires its efficacy by echoing, vibrating, and pulsating with the corporeal datum, or the realm of the pre-reflective depth of the world. This cross presents the possibility of refreshing and renewing the efficacy of a hackneyed code merging into the spectacle of autonomous referent-free signifiers by recovering its sensorial basis, i.e., by engaging with *fudo*.

Fudo and the dialectics of opposites

One significant principle in the operation of the cross as a code yet rooted in *fudo* is the dialectics of opposites that joins coldness and warmth, and darkness and brightness. Ando, the author of the cross, was aware of this dialectics, as he wrote of *ma*, a character meaning "in-between" in the Sino-Japanese linguistic tradition. Quoting Ando,

> The gap between elements colliding in opposition must be opened. This gap—the *ma* concept peculiar to Japanese aesthetics is just such a place. *Ma* is never a peaceful golden mean, but a place of the harshest conflict. And it is with *ma* thus informed with harshness that I want to continue to try and provoke the human spirit.[24]

What is unique about Ando's sense of *ma* is its dialectical dimension between opposites, a dimension that was rarely discussed by other Japanese authors who commented on *ma*.[25] Thanks to this dialectical dimension, Ando's definition of *ma* is striking, as it is "a place of the harshest conflict," not "a peaceful golden mean." It maintains the opposites in a contrasted balance, rather than formulating a third synthesis. Put differently, what is in operation is a unique sense of a dialectical balance charged with the energy of creation that emerges from the very confrontation itself. The character of each is augmented precisely because of its contextual reciprocity with its opposite, defining this contrasted balance to be the most effective form of joining, or an inseparable union. The simultaneous awareness of opposing qualities provokes and stimulates the human spirit. The space of in-between is thus not a space of harmony, but that of conflicts where contradictions are gathered together. This space is not simply the space of the beautiful, but that of unprecedented perceptual intensity.

However, Ando's joining of coldness and warmth itself should be understood not as an intellectual fabrication, but as rooted in the Japanese *fudo*. In this regard, Watsuji's distinctive sense of the balance between opposites operates as a primary reference. "The bamboo, a native of the tropics, covered in snow"[26] is the emblem of the dialectics that brings together, and mediates between, opposites of coldness and warmth (Figure 4.8). The extremes of the humid heat of the summer and the bone-chilling cold of the winter cultivate a common sensitivity of the Japanese to a balance between two extreme conditions. This balance is not intended to have coldness and warmth cancel each other out in a kind of zero-sum game, but to formulate a unique synthesis in which the oppositional confrontation between the two is maintained and augmented.[27] This dialectical encounter brings together opposite qualities and differences to form a higher level of accord. The opposing qualities such as softness and hardness, coldness and warmth, smoothness and roughness are joined together in the formula of "'dependent origination,' or, even preferably, 'co-dependent origination.'"[28] This "biconditional symmetry," "simultaneity, and biconditionality, of opposites without their higher synthesis"[29] aims at embodying a higher level of symmetry emerging out of the disposition of asymmetrical qualities.[30]

While discussing the significance of the Japanese garden, Watsuji further clarified the significance of this dialectics. He wrote,

> The Japanese garden between the soft, undulating moss and the hard stepping-stones. They create a contrast between, on one hand, the stepping-stone, their cutting, shape, and placement—for even when they make the stones square with a flat surface it is to express this contrast—and, on the other hand, the soft, flowing moss; but it is not some kind of academic "symmetry." . . . not one of geometrical proportion, but, rather, a harmonization of forces which appeals to our sensibilities—what I would call an accord of "spirit."[31]

The artist of a Japanese garden positions things in such a way that their qualities create a coordinated balance. In this fashion, the garden "brings into special focus the *underlying relatedness* of things, the mutuality that exists in spite of differences between hard and soft, great and small, and observer and observed."[32] It is the metaphoricity that sees the common ground between incompatibles not because of their explicitly formal similarity, but in spite of their apparent differences. The hardness of the stepping-stone in a Zen garden is hard because of the softness of the moss that surrounds the stone. They enliven each other not because of their formal similarities, but because of their relatedness that paradoxically emerges from their differences.[33]

Dialectics of opposites and human praxis

Regarding the dialectics of opposites that emerges from *fudo*, there is one significant fact to note: the coordination of different qualities is not for the sake of aesthetic diversity, but for the sake of augmenting human situations. In other words, this dialectic is destined not towards a higher level of esoteric formal play, but for the solidarity and augmentation of human praxis. The ritualistic procession attracted magnetically to the cross of light in the midst of coldness is a good example of this role of the dialectics.

Another example is again Watsuji's discussion of the sensorial dialectics in the Japanese garden. The accord of spirit such as the correspondence between stone pavement and soft moss

FIGURE 4.8 Bamboos covered in snow 2 (photo by Dongwook Ma, courtesy of the photographer)

in the Japanese garden path called *ro⁻ji* is not a mysterious formal play. Before it is a play, its significance is found in its effectuating human praxis of, for instance, the ritualistic procession towards the tea room. Put differently, the *ro⁻ji* does not present a meaningless concatenation of sensorial qualities; it constitutes a preliminary sensorial ensemble that encourages and augments specific postures, movements and gestures. One's careful stepping on the stone to maintain balance completes itself when the body feels the stone's hardness on the sole of the foot. The adamant resistance of the stone to the gravity of the body in turn gives firmness to its vertical posture that is temporarily, yet with full trust, resting on it. The softness of the moss covering the lanterns is not simply visual, either. The visual perception comes to be intertwined in and through the body with the tactile hardness of the stone in order to augment the stone's firmness and to complete the solidity of the vertical posture. Here, the visual and the tactile come to reciprocate each other, forming an ensemble not only for sensorial richness but also for the trustworthiness of the vertical posture. At the moment of voluntarily risking this erect solidity, one puts forth his footing to the interval between stepping stones. The alternation between the vertical stillness and its kinetic negation in the interval embodies the rhythm of the garden articulated, in Kakuzo Okakura's (1862–1913) characterization, in irregular regularity.[34]

Another example of the dialectics that joins differences to set up underlying relatedness for the augmentation of human praxis is the notion of "internal measure" by David Leatherbarrow.[35] By taking an urban restaurant in a European street as an example, Leatherbarrow analyzed the elements that participated in the formation of the setting—the large expanse of glass on the street side, along which a low and long table for the display of fruits is located; the frosted and square panes of glass framed within dark wooden lumber on the other side where dining tables stand—these both work together. Transparent and translucent are reciprocal. Low and high are reciprocal. Long and short are reciprocal. One party has to acknowledge its opposite as the dialogic partner for the enhancement of its performance. One does not stand alone for its efficacy. Transparency without translucency is dulled in its performance. A long expanse of transparent glass without a short breadth of translucent frosted glass is not efficient. The long, low display table acquires its identity through its differences with the standing, square dining table. The character of the restaurant, not as, for instance, a cafeteria, is in exact proportionate balance between these opposites in reference to human praxis—their coupling in such a way that the dining table is properly situated next to the frosted glass, while the display table is properly situated next to the transparent glass. Beyond this set of oppositional relationships within the restaurant is the context of the city, or the street in this case, toward which a display table is positioned, while the dining table is placed back in the depths of the restaurant. In this proper balancing lies the economy of the setting, an economy that is different from a conventional conception that emphasizes universal saving of materials, capital and labor regardless of what type of setting one is dealing with. In this conception of economy, waste of resources such as materials, capital and labor indicates none other than the rupture of the balance.[36]

Inter-*fudos* and beyond regional confines

The next issue I'd like to discuss is what Colquhoun called the essentialist perspective of the identity of a region, a perspective with which Colquhoun criticized regionalism as anachronistic. Simply put, the question is how we shall understand the identity of a region. A position that sees the identity of a region as consisting in its specificity of vernacular architecture, folksongs, dancing, music, customs, and so forth more or less falls to the category of essentialism. As Colquhoun criticized, such conception of regional identity is susceptible to insulated conservative politics and is even anachronistic regarding the reality of the contemporary advanced societies that are more flowing, fluid and flexible.

Watsuji's manner of thinking about the environment retained the dimension of what could be called inter-*fudos*, or the dimension between one *fudo* and another, beyond being incarcerated within a *fudo*. This philosophy of the inter-*fudo* and its correlate dialectical notion of identity offers one possibility of apprehending regional identity from a different angle.

There is a critical point of difference between essentialism and the dialectical notion of identity. In the former, one is self-sufficient with no necessity to engage with the other. In contrast, the dialectical notion of identity is possible only when one is engaged with the other. Accordingly, identity is not in itself, but in its dialectical relationship with its opposite. Identities co-emerge through their mutual contrast. It is a logic which one may call the dialectics of contrasted balance between opposites. The quality a building seeks to embody is not complete, until the building engages with and embraces the opposite of the quality, until the building forms a dialectical relationship with what it is not. Extending this further, the identity of a region is not in itself, but in its relationship with what it is not.

This aspect relates to the reciprocity between different *fudos* as discussed above by referring to "the bamboo, a native of the tropics, covered in snow."[37] The gracious curvature of the bamboo, in contrast with the verticality of the bamboo in tropics, emerges from the encounter of two opposed *fudos*: one, tropics, and the other, frigidity. These two *fudos* are experienced seasonally in Japan—the extremes of the humid heat of the summer and the bone-chilling cold of winter. Watsuji's thinking here opens a possibility that goes beyond the philosophy of a *fudo*—that of the reciprocity of different *fudos* in a contrasted balance and their creative cultural products. This moment is also important for the reason that the awareness of different *fudos* allows for the discourse of the pubic beyond the communal as defined by the insularity of a *fudo*. In terms of subjectivity, this moment is also important, as it introduces a wanderer's point of view—one who left his or her own *fudo* in order to encounter its opposites. The *fudo* of a region is distinctive not because it is self-sufficient, but because of its relationship with others. Even when Watsuji's aim was to clarify what his own culture was by referring to the other, what is confirmed here is not necessarily the uniqueness of a culture with a coherent and inherent system of identity, but the dialectical structure of the identity in which one is present because of the other, or one comes to be clarified because of its engagement with the other. In order to explain this dimension of inter-*fudos*, I would like to revisit the following analogical formula Nobuo Kioka drew out from Watsuji's notion of *fudo*:[38]

> Monsoon: Submissive and Persevering = Desert: Confrontational and Willful = Meadow: Rational and Regular

Indeed, his classification of the climates of the world into three parts—monsoon, desert and meadow—correspond to the route of the trip that he embarked upon in order to study philosophy under the governmental auspices of the Ministry of Education. He left the port of Kobe on March 17, 1927. The ship traveled through the South China Sea, the Indian Ocean, the Arabian Sea and the Red Sea, and the cities where the ship docked along the way included Shanghai, Hong Kong, Penang, Colombo and Aden. From the Red Sea, the ship traveled through the Suez Canal and entered the Mediterranean Sea to arrive in Marseille. From Marseille, Watsuji took trains to Berlin. In addition, while studying in Germany, he traveled not only to various cities in Germany, but also to different parts of Europe including Italy, France and England.

This Watsuji who was exposed to different *fudos* is thus the subject of inter-*fudos*, as he was neither at the center nor at the periphery. An important point is that this transposition away from his own *fudo* operated as the opportunity for him to discover his own *fudo* through encountering different *fudos*. This distanciation relocates the self away from habitual familiarity to discover both what is familiar and what is foreign. Accordingly, in this analogical formula is a simultaneous discovery of my *fudo* and an other *fudo*. If each *fudo* is the metaphor of who one is, as Watsuji argued, then this simultaneous discovery of my *fudo* and an other *fudo* is equally a simultaneous discovery of "who I am" and "who the other is." In this mutuality emerges the submissiveness and perseverance of the monsoon and at the same time the confrontation and willfulness of the desert. This analogy is thus a logic of mutual origination and of de-centralization. This type of characterization is not that of essentialism, but that of oppositional reciprocity in which the identity of a particular is empty until it is coupled with its opposite.

The analogical formula is the logic of openness and multiplicity.[39] This is because it is not only about the monsoon, but also about the desert. Simultaneously, it is not only about the monsoon and the desert, but also about the meadow, allowing room for the invitation of other differences. Any centrality that may exist in the discussion of the monsoon alone or in the discussion of the monsoon and the desert is relentlessly shattered as a new difference is introduced. This analogy is then the logic of de-centralization that overcomes self-centeredness. Nullifying any authoritative center, the analogy is open constantly to differences. It is at this moment that one starts to see the public nature of Watsuji's philosophy beyond the confines of the communal of a *fudo*. Watsuji's philosophy offers a basis for the discourse of the public in distinction with the communal. It offers an opportunity for an individual who has been kept within a *fudo* to see a different *fudo* and the humanity of which it is a metaphor. This in turn operates again as an opportunity for her to discover who she is in a contrasted reciprocity with the other.

However, there is a more important point in regard to the nature of the simultaneous discovery of who I am and who the other is. One cannot overemphasize the significance of one's encounter with a different *fudo* in terms of formulating a mutual discovery of who I am and who the other is. However, this discovery is not merely about seeing who I am, but also about seeing who I could become. One discovers not only the other per se, but also the other as his own potential. As much as I am confined in a *fudo*, the discovery of the other as my unexplored potential operates as an opportunity to transcend the confines of the *fudo*; i.e., the communal. This is the moment when one becomes a subject of freedom beyond the insularity of a *fudo*. Confrontation and willfulness of a desert person stretches the spectrum of humanity for a monsoon person, and becomes his own possibility. This subject of inter-*fudos* is the subject who not only joins analogically different *fudos* and correlate facets of humanities, but also discovers the limit of the communal and the different types of humanities and related types of human living. The subject surpasses the communal to move towards the public, of which his encounter with the other that cannot be domesticated, framed and manipulated is essential. It is this dimension of freedom uncovered through an encounter with the other that defines Watsuji's philosophy to go beyond climatic or regional determinism.

The regional and the trans-regional

Watsuji's dialectics of *ma* and of the inter-*fudos* leads us to transcend the confines of regionalism. The consciousness of different *fudos* beyond the confines of a region defines architectural practice to be predicated upon the dialectics between the specificities of the region's *fudo* and the trans-regional concern that surpasses climatic idiosyncrasies. One architect who did think in this manner is Aalto, introduced earlier. As is well known, Aalto's architecture has been understood as an antidote for the universal abstract practice of modern architecture.[40] His architecture was seen as reflecting specificity of the regional topography, landscape and materials, along with an emphasis on tactility. While these characterizations are valid, Aalto's architecture was trans-regional, not in the sense of style but in the sense of the typicality of the human living against which a different expression acquires legibility and significance. He understood some of his projects from the framework of the human ideals shared between different climates and regions, on one hand, and on the other different expressions of the same ideals. One good example is Saynatsalo Town Hall (1952) in Finland (Figures 4.2, 4.3). When Aalto participated in the competition for this hall, he drew inspiration from Italian precedents, including the campo of Sienna. Aalto saw the town hall of Sienna as "the world's most beautiful and most famous town hall," and decided to emulate it.[41] Then, he adopted a courtyard because, "in parliament buildings and courthouses the court has preserved its inherited value from the time of ancient Crete, Greece and Rome to the Medieval and Renaissance periods."[42]

Despite the climatic difference between the Nordic city of Saynatsalo and Sienna, Aalto understood the task of creating a town hall as embodying the human ideal of democratic justice and collectivity, like the *prytaneion* (town hall) or the *bouleuterion* (council house) in the agora of Greek cities, the cradle of democracy. Aalto's creation of a raised platform in the form of a rectangular courtyard for the project secured a human stage of equality out of an irregular and sloped wilderness. This process of creation involved reshaping the hilly site, strategically positioning four wings of buildings, and designing the buildings in a manner that suited the climate of the Nordic region by, for example, exposing their bases to resist snow frost, which is a climatic problem critical in the region. The square form of Aalto's courtyard is homologous to the more or less circular form of the campo of Sienna, despite their different appearances. In a circle, no point marks the beginning or the end, defining itself as a perfection and an idealization of human gathering: this is the reason why some primitive tribes found in different parts of the world dance together in circles. Similarly, the square of the courtyard represents the removal of an unfair hierarchy among human beings, rendering them into equally dignified citizens of Saynatsalo. Accordingly, what is sustained through this process of cultivation is not so much nature as such or nature as the not-unlimited reservoir of raw materials and energy; rather, it is the human praxis whose typicality and ideality beyond regional idiosyncrasies is tested and reconfirmed through different natural and climatic conditions.

Aalto's conception of architecture based upon the same human ideal of democracy beyond different *fudos* and their particular expressions offers an opportunity for us to revisit the nature of identity in architectural creation. Aalto's case is not of essentialism—that the identity is within the *fudo* of the region—as it acknowledges the ideal of the human living that is commonly found beyond regional boundaries. This ideal for Aalto, assigned with the task of designing a town hall, was none other than the democratic manner of gathering among individuals of different thoughts, ideas, and values. What is intriguing in Aalto's approach is the relationship between human cultural intention and the given natural and climatic condition. The reshaping of the hill is not an anthropocentric destruction of what is given based on a narrow human interest; rather, it is a cultivation of the hill and the augmentation of its topographical prominence into an elevated platform for ideal human encounters. The courtyard's integration between the columnar projection of the topography—etymologically, "hill" is associated with the Latin word *columna*, meaning a projecting object, column and so forth—and the leveled flatness is the actualization of *terra firma*, or the ideal land for human habitation that is both raised and leveled, dry and solid. The hill as such that is separated from, and uncontaminated by this cultural praxis and human value system—or pure nature as *Ding an sich*—is an idea, a theoretical fabrication abstracted from this concrete event of cultivation, not vice-versa. A prominent topography comes into being and comes to be intelligible precisely because it coalesces with human praxis, and this coalescence is the primary concrete experience in one's relationship with the surroundings.

Type and differences

Another author who pursued the interest of the trans-regional shared human ideals and their particular expressions is Aldo Rossi (1931–97). Of particular interest is his notion of type. Type was narrowly framed in the contemporary discourse on architecture. One example is the perspective posed against type by a position called "populationist." In *Atlas of Novel Tectonics*, Jesse Reiser and Nanako Umemoto discuss "the error of the typologist" and endorse the position called "populationist." In deploying their argument, they quote the contradistinction between the typologist and the populationist defined by Ernst Mayer (1904–2005), a leading evolutionary biologist of the twentieth century, who states that "for the typologist the type (*eidos*) is real and the variation an illusion, while for the populationist, the type (the average) is an abstraction and only the variation is real."[43] Accordingly, for the typologist, whose interest is in abstracted essence, tangible variations appear as mere degradations. In contrast, for the populationist, the abstract universal eradicates individual differences and falls far short from the real.

Although intriguing, this argument recapitulates the debate between idealism and realism in Western thinking that dates from Greek philosophy. Plato's idealism, in which truth exists in a pre-existing universal, and Aristotle's empiricism, in which sense-perception leads to the recognition of the universal, are echoed in the typologist and populationist arguments. The populationists may argue that their position is more radical than Aristotle's empiricism. Despite the fact that Aristotle valued the particular as the gate to the universal, he bypassed it eventually in the process of apprehending what the entity is. Aristotle wrote that "though the act of sense-perception is of the particular, its content is universal—is man, for example not the man Callias."[44] In contrast, the populationist position maintains the side of the individual by proliferating discrete or serialized variations. Such variations are not simply copies of the universal. Rather, they belong to a completely new category, in which, according to Gilles Deleuze (1925–95), individual entities are "like false claimants, built on dissimilitude, implying a perversion, an essential turning away" from the universal.[45] However, like Plato's idealism, this celebration of heterogeneity by the populationist does not resolve the presumed antagonistic relationship between the universal and the particular.

In order to resolve this conundrum, one has to stand on a different tradition, of which Watsuji is a distinctive thinker. Watsuji's manner of thinking that sees reciprocity between opposites and multiple differences is predicated upon the notion of emptiness, a concrete universal that originates from the ancient Indian philosophy of *sunyata* and that was later creatively revived in Japan during the first half of the twentieth century.[46] Overcoming the idea of the universal as the abstracted denominator of things, Watsuji articulated emptiness as the concrete universal from which the individual differences emerge in their unmitigated particularity. This emptiness, the ultimate *eidos*, was a topos in which beings emerge, exist and evaporate.[47] The entity and its opposite are intertwined through the principle of inverse correspondence, a higher level of accord that emerges from the disposition of asymmetrical qualities. Put differently, Watsuji's logic formulates a contradictory synthesis operating on a deeper level of intuition that sees relatedness between contrasting elements.[48] Because of this dependence of one upon another, Watsuji endorsed the principle of impermanence, while rejecting the self-sufficiency of being itself. The impermanence of identity should be understood not as the deprivation of identity, but as a dialectical openness and capacity through which identities co-emerge in temporality.

In defining Rossi's type in a manner that is distinguishable from the type as criticized by the populationist, this notion of concrete universal is conducive. Type was defined by Rossi as a constant, structuring principle. He further claimed that "no type can be identified with only one form, even if all architectural forms are reducible to types."[49] At first glance, with this statement, Rossi appears to have avowed a potential affinity to what Reiser and Umemoto called typologist. Rossi seems to have emphasized the principle of logical reduction of particular buildings to define their type. I believe, however, it is equally possible to interpret Rossi's statement in a way that is in contrast to the typologist position. The interpretation is this: Type is a common ground that allows the emergence of different forms and expressions, rather than a logical abstraction posterior to the formation of particular forms. This type is rooted in the pre-formal, situational praxis of human life, as Rossi wrote that "a particular type was associated with *a form* and *a way of life*, although its specific shape varied widely from society to society."[50] Once more, there is a degree of ambiguity in apprehending this passage. At the moment when Rossi coupled the idea of type with "a form," as if a type were again a special form abstracted from particular forms, I believe he confused readers, revealing a moot point in his theory of typology. However, at the moment when he coupled type with "a way of life," or the situations of human dwelling, he reassured type to be the permanent background against which and thanks to which particular forms emerge with their expressive distinctiveness. Extending this point on the connection between type and human life, type is none other than the pre-formal and pre-visual ideals such as authority and exaltation, equality in democracy, co-presence between collectivity and individuality, and enduring conditions of humanity, such as birth and death, finitude and infinity, and temporality and eternity. It is these ideals and conditions that tangible and particular expressions of architecture seek to embody. Accordingly, the task of design is to articulate a human ideal like equality. A human ideal is not what one can invent; rather, it is pre-given. However, its particular design that embodies an ideal is an invention.[51]

For Rossi, if a building is to acquire the status of a monument in the city, the core of the building should be somehow empty. The core in this case does not mean the plumbing system, structure, circulation, corridor, or ducts and shafts. Rather, it means the capacity and openness of the building so that it may operate as an ability to accept a performance that was not intended at the moment of its original conception. A monumental building is first and foremost a capacity to modify itself in order to accommodate different performances over time. For Rossi, the human history is filled with examples of this openness of a monument, like the Roman basilica, a legal court for civic matters that was adopted to realize the early Christian church. Rossi wrote, "A monument's persistence or permanence is a result of its capacity to constitute the city, its history and art, its being and memory."[52] Monumental buildings are enduring elements in the city, not because they never change, but because they do change, yet in the fashion of maintaining sameness. A monument emerges as such out of the dialectic between different phases of its performances, phases arrayed over the passage of time. From a diametrically opposite perspective, without changes over time, paradoxically, there is no permanence. The permanence of a monument cannot be revealed unless time is operating to create differences. In this way, a monument joins permanence and temporality together.

There is, however, a point that needs to be clarified further regarding the monument as capacity. The reason a building can operate as a capacity to modify itself in order to accept a different performance is because the building is *typologically* suitable for the change. The Roman basilica and the Christian church share the common ground of the axial progression with the raised podium at its terminus.[53] The reason the Roman basilica can operate as a Christian church of worship is because both buildings seek to embody authority and exaltation. It is now clear that what is persistent is not necessarily the *form* of the monument, even though Rossi sometimes confusingly implied this,[54] but the type of which the monument is an embodiment and against which different phases of the monument is revealed. A type is then "an atemporal backdrop that allows existing buildings to perform their changing roles."[55] Extending this argument further, a type is a backdrop that allows different forms in different periods and in different societies to come to significance. Stating from a different angle, a type is trans-regional, as well as transcendental of time. It is also possible to argue that local conditions, including its natural and climatic idiosyncrasies and variableness and conditions that are specific to a given moment are not simply an obstacle to overcome in realizing a type, but are instead an agency through and against which the typicality of human praxis beyond individual regions is tested and reconfirmed.

In Rossi's urban examples, buildings of the circular configuration such as the Coliseum and medieval towns were often introduced to illustrate his point on monument (Figures 4.9, 4.10). While Rossi did not fully clarify what kind of ideal the circular configuration intends to embody, I believe that it was Aldo van Eyck (1918–99) who clarified its typological value contextualized in human living with a couple of simple diagrams. As a member of Team X, van Eyck sought to transcend the categorical and mono-dimensional comprehension of the human being in high modernism. In this process, he presented the ideas of "poly-centric space" and "twin-phenomena." One example of these ideas was the duality the circular configuration embodies. The uniqueness of the circular configuration comes from the fact that its rim embodies the duality between the centrality of looking inward to find the communal center and the peripherality of looking outwards until one finds the distant horizon (Figure 4.11). It was neither about the center nor about the horizon, but their co-presence. As if confirming Rossi's claim that type emerges from human life, the circular configuration was observed in the manner in which a primitive tribe like the Dogon, a cliff-dwelling aborigine residing in southeastern Mali and

FIGURE 4.9 Coliseum as an example of a circular building (photo by author)

FIGURE 4.10 Market transformed from an amphitheater, Rucca, Italy (© minniemouseaunt, source: flickr.com)

Burkina Faso in Northern Africa, danced together (Figure 4.12). It was not that the circle was existent first, and then the tribe sought to tailor their dancing pattern to the geometry. Rather, the circle emerges out of the pattern of the dancing that embodies in its circular configuration the democratic ideal of nobody standing at the front or the ending tail. In turn, the circle operates as an idealized image of the human relationship because there is no moment of dancing in

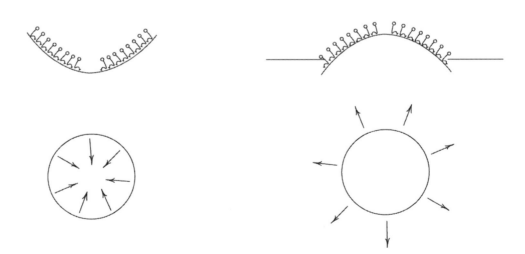

FIGURE 4.11 Aldo van Eyck, diagram of the duality of the circle (redrawn by Jihwan Choi based upon Aldo van Eyck, *Aldo van Eyck's Works*, compilation by Vincent Ligtelijn, trans. into English by Gregory Ball, Basel, Boston, Berlin: Birkhouser, 1999, pp. 292–3)

FIGURE 4.12 Aldo van Eyck, Dogen tribe dancing together (source: Aldo van Eyck, *Aldo van Eyck's Works*, compilation by Vincent Ligtelijn, trans. into English by Gregory Ball, Basel, Boston, Berlin: Birkhouser, 1999, p. 13)

which the co-presence between individuality and collectivity, and the co-presence between equality and leadership, is realized in perfection. Some parts are projecting, and other parts, indented. The circle operates as the ideal, again like the limit point towards which all dancing gatherings progress.

The rim of the circle where the polarity between center and horizon is operating is an example of the "in-between" in van Eyck's term. And, I believe the zone of in-between in van Eyck's architecture is the very place upon where the dialectic of opposites I discussed previously is constructed, a dialectic unique to the philosophy of Watsuji, as well as other East Asian thinkers. Like the dialectic of the resonance of opposites, the zone of in-between does not neutralize differences, in which case it simply succumbs to becoming another single entity or category, but maintains and sustains their simultaneous presence—"inwardness versus outwardness," "centrality versus peripherality," "protected versus open," "public versus private," "house versus city," "inside versus outside," and "bounded versus unbounded." This experiential intermediary zone where opposites exist without any explicit and reified formalistic synthesis, according to van Eyck, allows "'simultaneous awareness' of what is significant on either side."[56] He further wrote "an in-between place in this sense provides the common ground where conflicting polarities are reconciled and again become twin phenomena."[57] All the pairs co-present in the space of in-between in van Eyck's practice and theory, such as "the protected versus the open," are in various degrees the formal and spatial expressions of the dynamic between the communal and the individual who retains freedom to leave the communal in order to explore the open arena for potential human relationships. It is in this context that, in his "The Otterlo Circle," presented in 1959 at the CIAM Meeting in Otterlo, The Netherlands, van Eyck claimed that the task of architecture and urban design lie in creating a design "for each man and all men," and for "the individual and society." In this regard, good architecture does not impose one meaning over the other—for instance, it does not impose individuality over collectivity or peripherality over centrality—but lays out a platform on which the contrasting values are co-present.

There are various lessons one can glean from this notion of type from the perspective of sustainability. A building survives the test of time because it participates in the articulation of the human ideal and is thus typologically successful. Such a building must be apprehended not as a form but as a capacity to accommodate different situations and programs. What makes one's building sustainable beyond his or her life-span depends on to what degree the building participates in the articulation of human ideals. From the perspective of typology, a sustainable building is not merely about practical matters such as recycling of the materials and spaces of an old building; it is concerned with its role as a capacity to accommodate different programs over time precisely because it is of a human ideal such as the balance between the individual and the collective. This is the sustainability of human artifacts and ultimately the sustainability of humanity.

Notes

1 Kenneth Frampton, "Towards a Critical Regionalism: Six Points for an Architecture of Resistance," in ed. Hal Foster, *The Anti-Aesthetic, Essays on Postmodern Culture*, New York: The New Press, 1983, p. 25.
2 Ibid.
3 Ibid., p. 29.
4 Ibid., p. 28.
5 Ibid., p. 28.
6 Ibid., p. 29.
7 Tetsuro Watsuji, *A Climate: A Philosophical Study*, trans. Geoffrey Bownas, Ministry of Education Printing Bureau, 1961, p. 6.
8 Ibid., p. 6.
9 Ibid.
10 For instance, in his criticism of vision-dominated architecture, Juhani Pallasmaa illuminates multi-sensorial experience. However, his discussion of sensation remains largely at the level of the sensation of the individual. Juhani Pallasmaa, *The Eyes of the Skin: Architecture and the Senses*, Chichester: Wiley-Academy; Hoboken, NJ: John Wiley & Sons, 2005.
11 Tetsuro Watsuj, *Watsuji Tetsuro's Rinrigaku Ethics in Japan*, trans. Yamamoto Seisaku and Robert E. Carter, Albany: State University of New York, 1996, p. 17.
12 Ibid., p. 18.
13 Alan Colquhoun, "The Concept of Regionalism." in *Postcolonial Spaces*, ed. G.B. Nalbantoglu and C.T. Wong, New York: Princeton Architectural Press, 1997, p. 16.
14 Ibid., p. 15.
15 Ibid., p. 18.

16 Ibid., p. 17.
17 Ibid.
18 Ibid., p. 22.
19 Ibid.
20 Ibid., p. 23.
21 Tsuyoshi Hiramatsu, *Hikarino Kyokai: Ando Tadao no Genba*, Tokyo: Kenchikushiryo kenkyusha, 2000, pp. 315–17.
22 Regarding the dialectics embodied in the cross between the iconic and the phenomenal, *see* Jin Baek, *Nothingness: Tadao Ando's Christian Sacred Space*, London and New York: Routledge, 2009.
23 Acts 2:2.
24 Tadao Ando, "Thinking in *Ma*, Opening *Ma*," *El Croqui 58, Tadao Ando 1989/1992*, Madrid: El Croquis Editorial, 1993, p. 7.
25 As a matter of fact, the discussion of *ma* itself is not new in Japanese architecture. In architecture, *ma* has been one of the most celebrated concepts in explicating contemporary Japanese architecture. Since its appearance in the journal *Kenchiku Bunka* in 1963 and the book *Nihon no Tōshi Kūkan* in 1968, *ma* has been characterized as a unique Japanese aesthetic concept whose expressions are found on the stage of the *Noh* theatre, the board of the game *Go*, and the plans of Buddhist temples. The 1978 *Ma: Space–Time in Japan*, a ground-breaking exhibition organized by Arata Isozaki, which traveled to Paris and New York, and numerous writings on *ma* by Isozaki himself, Kisho Kurokawa, Fumihiko Maki, Teiji Itoh and others, stand behind the intensification of this authorized characterization. However, it is Ando who presented a dialectical notion of *ma*.
26 Tetsuro Watsuji, *A Climate: A Philosophical Study*, p. 135.
27 Although tangentially affiliated, this logic of the dialectical reciprocity is what defines Watsuji to be part of the Kyoto Philosophical School led by Kitaro Nishida. Masao Abe, "Non-Being and *Mu*: the Metaphysical Nature of Negativity in the East and West," *Religious Studies*, vol. 11, no. 2 (June 1975): 186.
28 Ibid.
29 David A. Dilworth, Introduction and postscript in Nishida Kitaro, *Last Writings: Nothingness and the Religious Worldview*, pp. 5–6, 130–1.
30 This dialectical logic should not be misunderstood as indicating a middle ground between the two co-emerging identities. This type of dialectic is not "dialectical (sublational) in a Platonic or Hegelian sense; . . . it does not postulate another level of being or noematic determination." Borrowing an example given by Nishida, it does not mean to synthesize gray out of white and black. This kind of synthesis merely produces another static entity, which loses the dialectical, tangible, and living creative energy emanating from the juxtaposed, yet inseparable, synthesis of the two opposites. In contrast, the two co-originating identities in this dialectic are intertwined through the logic of inverse correspondence. This dialectic operates through a deeper level of intuition which sees relatedness between contrasting elements. This intuition opens the possibility of defining connectedness, or continuity, not as the matter of expansive homogenous assimilation, but as the matter of discontinuous junctures. Ibid.; Kitaro Nishida, *Fundamental Problems of Philosophy, the World of Action and the Dialectical World*, trans. David A. Dilworth, Tokyo: Sophia University, 1970, p. 22.
31 Tetsuro Watsuji, *A Climate: A Philosophical Study*, pp. 191–3 (translation as found in William LaFleur, "Buddhist Emptiness in the Ethics and Aesthetics of Watsuji Tetsuro," *Religious Studies*, vol. 14, no. 2 (June 1978): 246.
32 William LaFleur, "Buddhist Emptiness in the Ethics and Aesthetics of Watsuji Tetsuro," *Religious Studies*, vol. 14, no. 2 (June 1978): 247 (LaFleur's italicization).
33 A phenomenon like this is also found in *sumie* painting. First of all, LaFleur cautions one not to see the large, unpainted space in a *sumie* painting as corresponding to Buddhist emptiness. For him, this mistaken view originates from "a facile mimeticism but would also involve a fundamental misunderstanding of the meaning of emptiness." The value of the void is "not that it makes palpable and concrete something metaphysical called 'non-being' but that it operates to make possible a series of relationships and reciprocities." A *sumie* painting thus presents a harmony not of formal symmetry, but of reciprocity between the void and, for instance, a dark silhouette of a wagtail at the bottom of the canvas. The void allows to be operable the imagination that penetrates relatedness and metaphorical common ground among the seemingly unrelated, and even conflicting entities. On these grounds, LaFleur rejects any of the two mistaken positions—one, emphasizing being and the other emphasizing non-being—in favor of the reciprocity of "not being one without the other." Ibid.
34 Kakauzo Okakura, *The Book of Tea*, New York: Dover Publications, 1964, p. 34.

35 David Leatherbarrow, "Architecture, Ecology, and Ethics," *Heaven and Earth, Festschrift to Honor Karsten Harries*, vol. 12, no. 1 (August 2007).

36 Ibid.

37 Tetsuro Watsuji, *A Climate: A Philosophical Study*, p. 135.

38 Nobuo Kioka, *Fudo no ronri: chiri tetsugaku eno michi*, Kyoto: Minerubashobo, 2011, p. 320.

39 Ibid., p. 312.

40 Since the inclusion of Aalto's architecture in Siegfried Gideon's second edition of *Space, Time and Architecture: The Growth of a New Tradition* (1949), Aalto's architecture had been positively cited during the post-war period as an example of overcoming functional and mono-dimensional modernism in architectural movements such as Kenneth Frampton's Critical Regionalism and publications such as Robert Venturi's *Complexity and Contradiction in Architecture* (1966).

41 Richard Weston, *Alvar Aalto*, London: Phaidon Press, 1996, p. 137.

42 Ibid.

43 Jesse Reiser and Nanako Umemoto, *Atlas of Novel Tectonics*, New York: Princeton Architectural Press, 2006, p. 226.

44 Aristotle, *Posterior Analytics*, Bk. II, ch. 19, 100b, 15–18, in *The Basic Works of Aristotle*, ed. Richard McKeon, New York: Random House, 1941, p. 185; Robert E. Carter, *The Nothingness beyond God: An Introduction to the Philosophy of Nishida Kitaro*, St. Paul, MN.: Paragon House, 1997, pp. 22–33.

45 Gilles Deleuze, "Plato and Simulacrum," trans. Rosalind Krauss, October 27 (Winter 1983): 47.

46 The philosophy of emptiness can be traced to the ancient Indian philosophy of *sunyata*, or emptiness. Later, Acharya Nagarjuna (c.150–250), the founder of the Madhyamaka School of Mahayana Buddhism, introduced emptiness to Buddhism in the process of solidifying Buddhism's key doctrines such as "no-self" and "dependent origination." The literature on Nāgārjuna's argument is numerous. One example would be the following offered by William LaFleur:

> Nagarjuna's philosophical enterprise was directed to the rigorous analysis of entities which some-one might somehow assume to have *svabhāva*, self-existent reality or existence in and of itself. Nagarjuna radically rejected any such possibility and attempted to demonstrate that each and every entity was "empty" of such self-existence. Another term, then, for this would be "dependent origination," or, even preferably, "co-dependent origination."

This logic of "co-dependent origination" joining differences to see their symmetrical reciprocity is the foundation for the notion of emptiness of the Kyoto Philosophical School led by Kitaro Nishida (1870–1945). Watsuji himself, as LaFleur argued, was part of this tradition, despite the fact that he was rather tangentially connected with the School. William LaFleur, "Buddhist Emptiness in the Ethics and Aesthetics of Watsuji Tetsuro," p. 244.

47 Emptiness is often understood as non-existence, a void that is symptomatic of a predominant fixation on objects. In contrast, the emptiness of the Kyoto Philosophical School is neither nothing, nor the suffocating void of limitless expansion in which things are at best desolately scattered. Rather, it is the ultimate foundation of reality that transcends ideas of "being" and "non-being." Subsequently, what is operating in emptiness is a double negation: the negation of being, which leads to non-being, and the negation of non-being. The second negation does not amount to being, which would be the case in formal logic. Instead, according to Nishida, it leads to the awareness of a horizon where the confrontation between being and non-being is transcended in favor of their co-emergence. Kitaro Nishida, *Complete Works (Nishida Kitaro zenshu)*, Tokyo: Iwanami shoten, 1947, vol. 4, pp. 217–19, 229–31.

48 Kitaro Nishida, *Fundamental Problems of Philosophy, the World of Action and the Dialectical World*, trans. David A. Dilworth, Tokyo: Sophia University, 1970, p. 22.

49 Aldo Rossi, *The Architecture of the City*, Cambridge, MA.; London: MIT Press, 1984, p. 41.

50 Ibid., p. 40 (my italicization).

51 David Leatherbarrow, *The Roots of Architectural Invention: Site, Enclosure, Materials*, Cambridge; New York: Cambridge University Press, 1993, p. 75.

52 Aldo Rossi, *The Architecture of the City*, Cambridge, MA.; London: MIT Press, 1984, p. 60.

53 David Leatherbarrow, *The Roots of Architectural Invention: Site, Enclosure, Materials*, p. 76.

54 For this ambiguous point latent in Rossi's typology, see David Leatherbarrow, *The Roots of Architectural Invention: Site, Enclosure, Materials*, p. 72.

55 Ibid., p. 71.
56 Aldo van Eyck, *Aldo van Eyck's Works*, compilation by Vincent Ligtelijn, trans. into English by Gregory Ball, Basel; Boston; Berlin: Birkhouser, 1999, p. 89.
57 Ibid.

CONCLUSION

In order to avoid causing any further environmental deterioration sustainability instructs us to discover and utilize new resources of energy, in particular renewable elements such as light, wind and rainwater. There was initially not much of the need to pay attention to these natural elements, because the earth had operated as an abundant storehouse. In addition, their exceptional ontological condition as '*ex-stasis*'—a condition of not having fixed profiles and being in a constant state of fluidity and unboundedness—made the framing and handling of them difficult. With the increasing awareness of a potential environmental debacle, however, we now frame them from the perspective of their capacity to produce energy with no side effects of pollution. Is this attitude still not the attitude that conceived nature as the storehouse of materials and resources? This attitude that conceives climatic elements as non–polluting sources of energy has often been justified by the perspective of self-preservation of the human being that aims to continue his or her life by propitiating nature. In order to overcome this kind of uncouth perspective of sustainability, we need to understand that the shortage of energy itself is not the gist of the problem: it is merely the result of our relationship with the surrounding things and our attitude towards the environment. In this context, we need to reflect upon the hegemonic attitude we have in the process of transforming the world into a storehouse of resources, a storehouse that can be appropriated at the whims of the human being seeking production, profits and materialistic affluence. In other words, a fundamental question we need to pose as to the current crisis is not so much about energy than it is about the relationship we have had and have with the environment. While developing techniques to squeeze energy from natural elements, a more fundamental inquiry into the relationship between ourselves and climatic elements must be simultaneously conducted. This also means that instead of presupposing that we all know what climate means for us at the moment due to the series of extensive scientific analyses that have provided copious data, it is time to inquire into the meaning of climate itself. It is in this context that we need to revisit the notion of *fudo* as proposed by Tetsuro Watsuji (1889–1960).

There are three aspects that distinguish Watsuji's theory of *fudo* from traditional climatology: the metaphor of subjectivity, the agency of the collective in the form of the dialectics of opposites, and lastly the dimension of the inter-*fudos*. Regarding the first aspect, Watsuji's interpretation of *fudo* as the metaphor of subjectivity is contradistinctive to the position of the traditional climatology. In the latter, the interest consists of how natural features and phenomena affect the way people live. It is thus predicated upon the mechanism of force and response—man either being subjected to, or overcoming, natural conditions. The climatology thus belongs to the arena of natural science. In contrast, Watsuji's climatology is concerned with how humanity and natural entities are intertwined and how humanity is invested in the qualities of natural entities. Its interest looks into how a natural phenomenon *appears* in concrete daily life. *Fudo* regards how natural phenomena are experienced in the human situational context. It rejects the metaphysical notions of nature such as "nature as such," "pure nature" and "nature as uncontaminated." The search for "nature as such" is indivisibly coupled with discontents of civilization such as pollution, waste, global warming, technological disasters and so forth. The mirage of "pure nature" is looked upon as the antithesis to civilization. In the midst of this hegemonic binary framework—nature and civilization—what is regrettably expunged is the dimension of culture and its creative cause.

Watsuji led his theory of *fudo* further when he demonstrated that natural phenomena and subjectivity are intertwined. A natural phenomenon does not merely stay in the outside of the self, but penetrates subjectivity and reciprocates with its various expressions. The endless expansion of sand in a desert comes into one's heart to imbue it with bleakness and to operate as the very image of bleakness as a phenomenon of subjectivity. The sea of sand as a form of natural landscape and bleakness as a form of the human heart reciprocate each other. It is in this context that Watsuji wrote, "The climatic character is the character of subjective human existence."[1] *Fudo* is consequently an agent for self-discovery. It is, stated Watsuji, "The agent by which human life is objectified, and it is here that man comprehends himself; there is self-discovery"[2] in *fudo*. "The bamboo, a native of the tropics, covered in snow,"[3] a landscape distinctive of a monsoon area where the tropical woody plant grows while placed at the same time under the influence of the Siberian freeze, is accordingly a metaphor for the human heart, or duality, a virtuous form of human character in East Asia that joins restrained calmness on the surface with an ever-burning passion inside. The dialectics of opposites between the two forces is a mirror for the dialectical ensemble of the human heart between passion and restraint.

The second distinctive aspect in Watsuji's theory of *fudo* is its inter-personal dimension. Watsuji pointed out the pervasive nature of *fudo*. The 'I' does not stand as an isolated or heroic independent entity. Rather, it is found in the middle of a climatic atmosphere such as coldness. What is further important is the fact that it is indeed not only the 'I' but also 'we' that is found in the middle of coldness. Different individuals come to be infected by the same atmosphere. Watsuji thus opened a room for the condition of what I would like to call "common subjectivity" that joins different 'I's into one. A mountain blast that fills up *my* heart with coldness makes indeed *our* hearts cold. In this common corporeal basis emerge expressions of distinctive identities such as the parent and the child in which the parent would look for a piece of clothing to cover up the child. Common subjectivity is the basis for the articulation of different identities, their roles and actions proper to distinctive roles. What is also important is to apprehend the fact that the self in the mode of common subjectivity is the self of act and creation. In other words, *fudo* is the agent by which not only the self but also the self-active human being is objectified.

In explicating this dimension of common subjectivity, Watsuji took up '*ex-sistere*,' or "standing-out," defining it as "to be out among other 'I's."[4] '*Ex-sistere*' leads Watsuji to go beyond the intentionality of "thinking of," which was still self-centered. The 'I' is thus already there, formulating a dialectical structure of the 'I' of here and the 'I' of there. The 'I' of there that is imbued with the quality of the atmosphere situates "there" as the locus of common subjectivity where the 'I' of there, 'you' of there, 'her' of there and so forth are present. Here emerges the ground for the formation of "a mutual relation that discovers ourselves in the cold"[5] and for the formation of collective measures in reference to climatic phenomena. *Fudo* functions in this manner as the agency for the formation of mutual relations. At this moment, self-enclosed individualism is overcome in favor of common subjectivity that cultivates collective cultural measures. These measures come into being not because of empathy, which still presupposes the centrality of the 'I' as the active party that projects a feeling, but because of the mutually reciprocal bond between different 'I's as situated in the same atmosphere and as affected and embraced by it. On account of this archaic bond in the human relationship mediated through *fudo*, Watsuji went so far as to state that "every trace of the notion of independent existence must be voided."[6] His view of the collective dimension of the human being is further confirmed through his philological study into *ningen*, or man in the Sino-Japanese linguistic tradition. Within the definition of "man," *gen* meaning "in-between" speaks of a dialectical whole. It is a whole of opposites (father/mother, parent/child, brother/sister . . .), confirming Nagarjuna's logic of co-dependent origination. One is there because of the other. One would not be present, if it were not for the other. The whole is the summation of this mutually inter-dependent and mutually negating series of relationships. Simultaneously, the relationship between the whole and the particulars itself is that of mutual negation and mutual interdependence. There is no whole unless these are contrasted particulars.

The third distinctive aspect of Watsuji's environmental philosophy to note is the dimension of the inter-*fudos*. Concerning this point, one should be reminded that Watsuji's theory of *fudo* would not have come into being if he had not embarked upon a trip to Europe from Kobe on March 17, 1927, in order to study philosophy under the governmental auspices of the Ministry of Education. This trip exposed Watsuji to diverse *fudos*. Indeed, his classification of the climates of the world into three types—monsoon, desert and meadow—correspond to the route of the travel. The ship traveled through the South China Sea, the Indian Ocean, the Arabian Sea and the Red Sea, and the cities where the ship docked along the way included Shanghai, Hong Kong, Penang, Colombo, and Aden. From the Red Sea, the ship traveled through the Suez Canal and entered the Mediterranean Sea to arrive in Marseille. From Marseille, Watsuji traveled by rail to Berlin. In addition, while studying in Germany, he traveled not only to various cities in Germany, but also to different parts of Europe including Italy, France and England.

Through his travels, Watsuji was able to acquire an awareness of the *fudo* of his own country. By engaging with others and by being outside of his own land, he became conscious of the characteristics of his own climate. By becoming imbued with the heat of the Indian Ocean, he became aware of the bone-chilling coldness of the Japanese winter. By being exposed to the carefree clarity of nature in Italy and Greece, he became aware of the uncontrollable jungles of Japan nurtured by a combination of heat and humidity in the summer. In England and Germany, according to Watsuji, a foggy day is succeeded by another. In Italy and Greece, a clear day is the norm. This monotony of the European climates—although others may find this characterization arguable—led Watsuji to become aware of the varieties of climatic conditions in Japan where high and varying levels of humidity combined with the sun brings about variegated nuances in the atmosphere throughout the day, month and year—"the cool of a summer's evening, for example, the freshness of the morning, the violent change, sufficient to bring a complete change of mood, between the noon warmth and the biting cold at sunset of an autumn day, the morning cold in winter, enough to shrivel the skin, and, after it, the balmy warmth of an Indian summer day."[7]

While the Watsuji of the homeland was not aware of the character of his own *fudo* and what aspect of humanity it is the metaphor of, the Watsuji en route to Europe was exposed to differences that enabled him to discover his own *fudo* and reflect upon its metaphorical nature. Hence, this process of self-discovery relied on the acknowledgment of others and their presence, which opened a dimension of the inter-*fudos*. For Watsuji, his trip to the Indian Ocean created a moment in which he was in this foreign ocean and in his homeland simultaneously through reminiscing. The Watsuji of the Indian Ocean and the Watsuji of his homeland from which he was temporarily dislocated was the very structure where he could reflect on what his *fudo* was like. To a degree, this is the logic of discovering who I am, or what my *fudo* is and what aspect of humanity it represents, by being engaged with others, their *fudos* and the types of humanity the *fudos* mirror. It is the logic of co-dependent origination, and thus that of decentralization. If the common subjectivity speaks of the communal embraced by the same *fudo* and the humanity it mirrors the dimension of the inter-*fudos* speaks of one leaving the interior of a *fudo* and is concerned with the public beyond the communal.

In this regard, it is worthwhile to pay attention to Watsuji's discussion of different *fudos* such as the monsoon, desert and the meadow, and the type of humanity each *fudo* is a metaphor for. For Watsuji, the monsoon is characterized by the combination between heat and humidity. Heat alone is bearable. Heat, if combined with humidity, however, becomes unbearable. Simultaneously, humidity energized by heat appears often as violent and destructive—typhoons, hurricanes, floods and so forth. Accordingly, the monsoon is apprehended dualistically: it is a blessing in terms of harvesting abundant rice, and simultaneously a curse for its violent behaviour. Watsuji claimed that man here appears submissive and persevering, waiting for the benevolence of nature. In contrast, the desert is anything but a form of natural benevolence: it is hot, harsh, tough and desolate, offering very little in terms of survival, as one has to constantly move around in search of water and grains. Life in the desert is thus confrontational and willful, as it is ingrained with a double battle—fighting with nature that provides little and fighting with other tribes to keep what little nature has given to him, his family and his tribe. In this culture surfaces the strongest form of the communal. Lastly, the meadow as exemplified by the landscapes of Italy and Greece is different from monsoon and desert. Here, there is no equivalent to the entangled jungle of monsoon. Its climatic pattern in which the summer is dry and the winter is a bit rainy gives full exuberance neither to weeds nor to crops, while not being as harsh and tough as the rugged reality of the desert. Thanks to low levels of humidity, its atmosphere is transparent. No turbulent storm, except sporadic sirocco, is experienced in the atmosphere. As though meticulously tended by a gardener, a natural element such as cypress grows geometrically on its own accord. It is not coincidental that within this transparent atmosphere emerged the notion of *theoria*, or the joy of seeing, as humidity fogs little and everything is visible. This atmosphere is further layered with the transparent logic of geometry based upon which things grow. Watsuji finally wrote that the mentality here is thus rational and regular.[8]

One could see these characterizations of the *fudos* and their correlate forms of humanity simply as another form of regional determinism. From the perspective of the inter-*fudos*, however, the matter is not this simple. According to Nobuo Kioka,[9] Watsuji's portrayal of the characteristics of the *fudos* and their correlate forms of humanity formulates a proportional relationship:

Monsoon: Submissive and Persevering = Desert: Confrontational and Willful = Meadow: Rational and Regular

What is in operation here is an analogy in which the meaning of one is dependent on the meanings of the other two. Again, it is only when one stands at the outside of one's own *fudo* that he or she is able to realize its nature. Accordingly, this is not simply a form of determinism. Rather it is a form of constant openness to differences. Put differently, the proportional relationship is constantly open to different *fudos* and the humanity they are a metaphor of. Watsuji's characterization is not that of essentialism, but a characterization through analogy and oppositional reciprocity. From the movement from one *fudo* to another, as implied in the formula, one indeed sees Watsuji along his route from one *fudo* to another, discovering his own *fudo* through encountering a different *fudo*. He himself is the subject of the inter-*fudos*, neither at the center, nor at the periphery. This series of movement is simultaneously a series of transposition of the location of the self, distancing the self from familiarity in order to discover both what is familiar and what is foreign. This simultaneous discovery of my *fudo* and an other *fudo* is a simultaneous discovery of "who I am" and "who the other is."

There is a point of utmost importance in this openness to different *fudos*. In encountering different *fudos* and the forms of humanity they mirror, I discover not only myself, or who I am, and who the others are, but also, the others as my own unexplored possibilities. I see my possibility beyond the confine of monsoon to become a desert person or a meadow person. In other words, I transcend the confine of the communal to emerge as a subject of freedom to explore a different possibility of who I am. Watsuji's philosophy is not that of fixity, but that of discovery and openness. This fact also confirms that Watsuji's philosophy is not a philosophy of climatic or regional determinism, but eventually of freedom and potentialities.

This philosophy of acknowledgement of the others and of freedom and potentialities functions as the basis for the apprehension of the relationship between the communal and the public. The communal whose distinctive form would be a village embraced within a single *fudo* is often characterized by a close bond between the *fudo*, on one hand, and, on the other, the industry, cuisine and culture. The communal is sustained often by internal rules of operation such as a hierarchy—prioritizing the whole, for example, the family over the individuals and the village over the villagers. In contrast, the public occurs at a moment when one seeks to move beyond the given *fudo* and its correlate society; it is a turning away from the protected interiority of the communal. The one who leaves the communal is the one who has awakened to the presence of the exterior, positioning one in a dynamic between belonging to a communal society and being free to come out of the society. The public thus lives on the volition to place oneself beyond the territory. Watsuji's subject of the inter-*fudos* is exactly this type of subject who stands in a public sphere. He or she is the one who negates the centralizing desire, who overcomes self-centeredness, and who finally moves into the interstitial space between different communities. It is also a place where a de-centralized individual encounters another de-centralized individual to experiment unconditioned possibilities and potentialities that may exist in the inter-personal to formulate an alternative society. At this moment, there emerges an ideal of the place of trans-*fudos*. This place operates as an agency that allows differences to emerge, as, for instance, a shared platform is the condition based upon which different heights are clarified, and that guarantees differences' mutual interactions. This place of trans-*fudos* is then the ethical place of shared human ideals, despite, and simultaneously on account of, the differences, such as democracy and equality that necessarily presupposes differences.

This work has explored the architectural significance of Watsuji's environmental thinking by conducting three independent studies: the nature of the spatial configuration of the Japanese vernacular residential architecture, of which Watsuji himself wrote; the environmental philosophy of Richard Neutra (1892–1970); and lastly, the discourse of regionalism and trans-regionalism in contemporary architecture. Regarding the first, Watsuji's interpretation of the spatiality of the Japanese house is the distinctive example of the linkage from the climatic to the inter-personal. While the first generation of architects in Japan devised a plan embodying privacy and its correlate ideology of the individual, along with blocking noise and clarifying functional divisions, Watsuji refreshed the significance of the flexibility of the Japanese house. "Selfless openness," with which Watsuji portrayed the spatiality of the Japanese vernacular house, is possible only when there arises the joining of different 'I's as standing in '*ex-sistere*' in the midst of a pervasive and encompassing climatic phenomenon. Characterizing the openness of the Japanese house with selflessness, self-apprehension and collectivity is profound; it modifies the dominant modernist view that the Japanese openness embodies functional flexibility and efficiency. It also gives rise to a lesson for contemporary residential architecture. The sustainable performance of Japanese houses in summer arises from the basis of collectivity, in which individuals are joined together to formulate a 'we.' Put differently, Watsuji's elucidation offers an opportunity for us to reflect upon our habitual emphasis on privacy embodied through the configuration of individual, separate rooms connected only through a corridor. Watsuji's *fudo* leads us to examine the way we formulate the relationship between man and climate; and whether we stick mechanically to privacy, not understanding the fact that the collectivity of, in Watsuji's words, "selfless openness" is the basis for a proper passive sustainable performance. For Watsuji, there is no such thing as a pure individual who would stay in an enclosed room with an air-conditioner. Rather, a true individual is an individual of *act*, one who joins himself or herself with other 'I's in the process of formulating a collective measure in response to a climatic phenomenon in which he or she is situated.

In comparison with the conventional regionalism that states that one must be sensitive to local qualities of light and wind, Neutra's residential and educational architecture addresses a different sense of climate and inter-personal linkage. It is also distinguished from what the positions critical of regionalism labeled as the negative instance of regionalism, which manipulates and combines images of local tradition only to become a nostalgic representation of what has been lost. Neutra's creation is concerned not with images but with the relationship between different elements of *fudo*. He understood the California desert from the perspective of invisible, yet palpable forces of *fudo* and seeks to recover a balance between them through active human intervention. Fire alone fails to survive, as wind is deficient. However, the exclusive combination of fire and wind, in particular, in the context of a desert is also dangerous, occasioning a need to introduce water into the formula. In this manner, the significance of Neutra's setting is dialectically and constantly open for the addition of opposites, rather than being pre-determined and fixed. For him, the significance of fire is not in itself, but is situational in reference to its relationship with what it is not, such as wind and water. Like the "bamboos covered in snow," a landscape that emerges from the dialectics of two opposite forces of tropical heat and Siberian cold, what is embedded in Neutra's residential setting is this very dialectics of opposite forces. Neutra's dialectical setting predicated upon a proportional coordination of fire, wind and water defines itself to be an inter-dependent network of mutually opposing differences. The formation of this fictive network gives a hint of the nature of a *cultural* creation, which is distinctive both from naturalism that believes in keeping nature as it is, and from civilization that instrumentalizes nature as a storehouse of exploitable resources. Distancing itself from these two extremes, the shaping of a dialectical network runs a middle path. This cultural creation respects what is given in the natural, such as heat and dryness—the qualities of fire, abundant in the desert—yet installs what is lacking in the natural concurrently, such as the calming power of water.

What further defines Neutra's creation to be *cultural* is the fact that the coordination of the balance between different qualities, the key for Neutra in any architectural endeavor, was meant to enhance human affairs. The encounters between fire and wind, and between fire and water were not esoteric formal plays, but were coalesced with the augmentation of primary human conditions. As a matter of fact, Neutra's continual effort to set up a right relationship among the fireplace, the window and the reflecting pool included another element of the human abode; i.e., a daybed as best represented by the living room in the Miller House. The anchoring of a human abode on a site for Neutra was thus a matter of restoring the balance among the primary elements. In this process, Neutra's anchoring was predicated upon a trans-regional perspective, in which what is dominant in a *fudo* must be modulated into a balance by encountering a character of a different *fudo*. It is significant to note that, for instance, the daybed was the essential locus for human gathering in the context of the family life. The corner where the daybed was situated was enshrouded in a shade in combination with a breeze, or was warmed up at night when the cold hit the desert outside. Borrowing the psychoanalytical jargon of which Neutra was quite dexterous, the daybed was not a melancholic, solitary appeasement of the lost thermal memory of the uterus, but the common sense of 'we' sharing a platform characterized atmospherically by the dialectical ensemble of fire, wind and water. For Neutra, the post-birth life initiated not the loss of the paradise, but the inter-personal discovery of "facing" the mother and the father, and other members of the family. Birth extends the physical and instinctual intimacy enveloping the fetus in the womb to different levels of the human relationship in the post-womb—filial, friendly, parental, pedagogical, erotic and so forth.

Neutra adopted the term empathy, or "in-feeling," in order to describe the nature of communication that takes place around the daybed. I believe, however, what Neutra sought to convey was indeed something different. The type of communication that he intended to convey is not, as in the theory of empathy, of one projecting a feeling into the other as if he or she was the center and the point of origination, but rather of one where both one and the other are penetrated by the same feeling. Before there is a projection, there is first an atmosphere that embraces both one and the other. As Neutra wrote, the atmosphere captures one and the other and embraces them as one, and flows freely from one heart to another, as if the atmosphere itself has its own life and way of penetrating human hearts. If empathy is a self-centered communication, what Neutra wrote of was a selfless communication, or a communication that operates before the formation of the consciousness of the self. While aiming at discussing something else, Neutra's vocabulary was still captured within the legacy of the Western intellectual history, in which the 'I' is a never-doubted *a priori* category. Watsuji's theory of communication is found more efficient in explicating Neutra's intention. Adopting Watsuji's '*ex-sistere*,' or "to be out among other 'I's," the 'I' exists not as the center or the point of origination for the projection of a feeling. Rather, the 'I' is thus already there, formulating a dialectical structure of the 'I' of here and the 'I' of there. As argued, the 'I' of there that is imbued with the quality of the atmosphere situates "there" as the locus of common subjectivity where the 'I' of there, 'you' of there, 'he' of there and so forth are present. Apathy, unrelatedness and strangeness are overcome to operate as the basis for speech, communication, consensus and act.

Lastly, Watsuji's *fudo* has a significant lesson for regionalism, and even for the antithetical criticism of regionalism. Watsuji's clarification of the link between the response to climatic conditions and the inter-personal overcomes the limit of the discourse of regionalism. As illuminated, in Watsuji's thinking, the common sensation of '*ex-sistere*,' or the 'I' that stands in the middle of a *fudo* along with the 'I's of the others, defines climate as the agency of the inter-personal.

In the phenomenon of self-apprehension in a milieu, the 'I' is joined with the other 'I's. Watsuji thus wrote that "it is in our relationship with the tyranny of nature that we first come to engage ourselves in joint measures to secure early protection from such tyranny."[10] Creations through the joining of different 'I's are the basis for what we call culture. Culture is none other than "an inheritance of self-apprehension accumulated over the years since the time of our ancestors."[11] Again, the "selfless openness" of the Japanese domestic space in response to the hot and humid climate is the epitome of a collective measure exemplifying the liaison between the response to climatic conditions and the inter-personal. In this manner, Watsuji's theory compensates for the theory of Critical Regionalism as theorized by Kenneth Frampton by clarifying the inter-relationship between the sensation of climatic elements and the situation of the inter-personal. This linkage between the sensational and the inter-personal saves regionalism from the cult of sensation such as aestheticized emphasis on tactility with no prospect for a higher ground of concrete daily human situations into which, for instance, a tactile experience is, and must be, tangentially sublimated.

It is also worthwhile noting how Watsuji's theory of *fudo* offers an aspect based upon which Alan Colquhoun's (1921–2012) criticism of regionalism could be modified. Colquhoun pointed out the conservative aspect of the communal leading in its extreme to an ultra-version that lays stress on racial purity. Regionalism in this case assumes an ideological role that supports the uniqueness of a community and her culture and even her superiority over other communities. The conception of identity in such regionalism is characterized as what Colquhoun called the essentialist model—that a culture has a core filled with a specific set of codes, customs, folk songs and so forth. Discussing climate as one of the primary factors in formulating the architecture of regionalism also suffers from this essentialist model, and is based upon a rigid and fixed relation-ship between cultural codes and regions. At the same time, while nothing is wrong with the position of regionalism in that architecture should be sensitive to a local identity by addressing climatic distinctiveness, in most cases "regional" is apprehended at the level of formal and tectonic features, features that are treated as images to be theatrically manipulated. Accordingly, for Colquhoun, discussion of regionalism in the contemporary post-industrial period, in which codes emancipated from regional bonds float around, is irrelevant and outdated.

At a theoretical level, the notion of identity as implied in Watsuji's theory of *fudo* escapes Colquhoun's criticism of essentialism. Watsuji's awareness of his own climate and thus of the identity of his region comes into being through his existence outside of his own climate. While keeping the notion of region, Watsuji's thinking opens a space between regions and a mutual reflection for the clarification of their identities. Even when Watsuji's aim was to clarify what his own culture was by referring to the other, what is confirmed here is not necessarily the unique-ness of a culture with a coherent and inherent system of identity, but the dialectical structure of the identity in which one is present because of the other, or one comes to be clarified because of its engagement with the other. Watsuji's environmental philosophy is accordingly based upon what could be called inter-*fudos*, or the interstitial dimension between one *fudo* and another, beyond being incarcerated within a *fudo*. This manner of apprehending the identity of a region corresponds to the logic of the dialectics of opposites in which distinctiveness of a climate is not in itself, but rather in its relationship with what it is not. The *fudo* of a region and its significance is distinguishing not because it is self-sufficiently so, but because of its relationship with others. Accordingly, identity is not in itself, but in its dialectical relationship with its opposite. Identities co-emerge through their mutual contrast.

One cannot overemphasize the significance of one's encounter with a different *fudo* in terms of formulating a mutual discovery of who I am and who the other is. As illuminated above, however, this discovery is not merely about seeing who I am but also about seeing who I could become. One discovers not only the other per se, but also the other as his own potential. As much as I am confined in a *fudo*, the discovery of the other as my unexplored potential operates as an opportunity to transcend the confines of the *fudo*; i.e., the communal. This is the moment when one becomes a subject of freedom beyond the insularity of a *fudo*. At this moment of co-emergence, the subject of the inter-*fudos* is fixed neither at the central hegemonic vantage point nor at the periphery. The confrontation and willfulness of a desert person stretches the spectrum of humanity for a monsoon person, operating as his own unexplored potential. This subject of inter-*fudos* is the subject who not only joins analogically different *fudos* and correlate facets of humanity, but also discovers the limit of the communal and the different types of humanity and related types of the human living. The subject surpasses the communal to move towards the public where his encounter with the other that cannot be domesticated, framed and manipulated. It is this dimension of freedom uncovered through an encounter with the other that defines Watsuji's philosophy to go beyond climatic or regional determinism.

At the level of practice, it still seems possible to argue for the codes that are universal yet based in the idiosyncrasy of different *fudos*. Tadao Ando's cross in the Church of the Light (1989) was a good example. The efficacy of light in a monsoon region where a high level of humidity fogs the atmosphere is always a challenge. In overcoming this condition of the local *fudo*, Ando excised the front wall in the shape of a cross to invite a direct sunlight, while darkening the remaining part of the church. He also polished the surface of the concrete walls inside to maximize their capacity to reflect light and thereby to maximize light's presence filling the darkness. His approach marks a great contrast with Kenzo Tange's (1913–2005) cross on the ceiling in St. Mary's Cathedral (1964) in Tokyo which invites an indirect light only to register a dull presence. On a dry winter's day during which a crispy atmosphere not dissimilar to that of humidity-free Greece is serendipitously felt from time to time, the cross is particularly efficacious. The one who has been instantly infected with the coldness of the space, constructed monolithically in concrete, is unconditionally attracted to the warmth of the light that comes in through the cross. This cross is qualitatively different from the signifier, which is informative and cerebral without any corporeal resonance with the perceiver and eventually develops into an empty one systematically emancipated from its referent. In other words, one's engagement with the cross does not yield a meaning of cerebral aridity, but acquires its efficacy by echoing, vibrating with, and pulsating with the corporeal datum, or the realm of the pre-reflective depth of the world. This cross renews the efficacy of a hackneyed code and even rootless floating signifier, if not dragged down to the level of kitsch, merging into the spectacle of autonomous, referent-free signifiers by recovering its sensorial basis; i.e., by engaging with *fudo*. The cross as the universal symbol of Christianity reinvigorates its significance by joining itself with the light of the local area.

In the efficacious presence of the cross of light, dialectics of opposites is the key. Darkness and light are joined to each other. Coldness and warmth are joined to each other. Theological significance comes to be intertwined with the dialectics to accommodate a human situation in which believers who have been enshrouded in darkness and coldness are to be unconditionally attracted to the brightness and warmth of the light. This interdependent network of opposites defines the meaning of an element such as darkness to be fictive, as the meaning is never fixed but is dialectically open to encounter its opposite. This dialectics, in which opposites correspond to each other for mutual identification and reinforcement (A = not A), breaks off at the moment in which trite perceptual experience defined by the transparency of the formal logic (A = A) dominates.

This dialectics of opposites gives a hint at the fact that the key to sustainability is not only the materialistic interest of saving resources, but apprehending the nature of involved situations and setting up of a proper relationship among elements that support the intended situations. The whole from which an atmosphere emerges is the coordinated summation of differences, a coordinated unity of differences. Economy, or sustainability, consists in none other than the proper distribution of the differences, and setting up a relationship among them in reference to human situations to be accommodated.

Watsuji's discussion of the inter-*fudos* is further significant in that it opens a theoretical space for the trans-regional aspect of human living; i.e., typicality of human praxis and its dialectical relationship with the local particulars, including its natural and climatic idiosyncrasy and variableness. Watsuji's swift intellectual trajectory from *fudo* that regards man's relationship with nature to ethics as the matter that regards the inter-personal relationship is, in a sense, indicative of his awakening into the significance of this trans-regional dimension. It is the dimension where the relationship between man and man acquires a kind of autonomy that is equipped with its ideal types of the human relationship—autonomy that takes a given *fudo* as a primary factor for its various particular expressions. The conception of architecture in this case is dualistic—the same human ideal, such as equality, beyond different *fudos* and its particular expressions. Subsequently, it challenges essentialism that the identity is within the *fudo* of the region, as it acknowledges the ideal of human living that is commonly found beyond regional boundaries. Alvar Aalto's (1898–1976) discussion of the role of the piazza in the historical continuity from Crete to the contemporary period is a good example for this trans-regional perspective of human living. The significance of the urban space consists in the enactment of an ideal human relationship in which differences in terms of sexes, thoughts, values, races and so forth are revealed, exposed, articulated, encountered, negotiated and synthesized. This encounter is thus embedded with the flowering of the potentials of the relationship such as the erotic, filial, parental, friendly, pedagogical and so forth. The common sensation that presupposes the shared corporeal datum of the human being beyond the differences seems to operate as a preordained basis on which differences could be gathered in the first place. This compassion of '*ex-sistere*,' mediated through climatic phenomena, functions as the ground for communication, such as gestures, greetings, conversation and speech, leading eventually to consensus and action. Watsuji's preferred format of this encounter that joins differences on the basis of a common sensation was the co-originating and co-dependent dialectic of opposites, in which one is never self-sufficient but is existent on account of its difference with the other, and in which one is dialectically conjoined with the others to implement a meaningful action.

Aldo Rossi's (1931–97) notion of type addresses the dimension of the trans-regional from a different angle. Distanced both from the conventional conception of type, such as the sorting of buildings based upon their functions, and from the accusation that type eradicates particularities, Rossi's type signifies a human constant that is expressed in different forms. Type is a common ground that allows for the emergence of different forms and expressions, rather than a logical abstraction posterior to the formation of particular forms. This type is rooted in the pre-formal, situational praxis of human life, crystallizing ideals such as authority and exaltation, equality in democracy, and co-presence between collectivity and individuality, and coping with enduring dualistic conditions of humanity such as birth and death, finitude and infinity, and temporality and eternity. A type is in this fashion trans-regional, as well as transcendental of time. For this reason, it operates as a permanent background against which and thanks to which particular forms acquire their expressive distinctiveness. It is in this context that, as David Leatherbarrow argued,[12] a type is not what one can invent; rather, it is pre-given. Its particular design that embodies an ideal, however, is an invention. Local conditions, including natural and climatic idiosyncrasy and variableness, and conditions that are specific to a given moment, are not simply an obstacle to overcome in realizing a type, but are instead an agency through and against which the typicality of human praxis beyond individual regions is tested and reconfirmed.

Type refreshes the significance of human artifacts from the viewpoint of sustainability. A building that embodies a type such as exaltation is often successful in accommodating a program that was not originally intended for. Such a building grows into a monument. In other words, type defines a building to be a capacity to accept different performances, in the process of which the building acquires the status of a monument. The Roman basilica, a legal court for civic matters, which was adopted for the early Christian church, is an example. Despite the programmatic differences, the Roman basilica and the Christian church share the common ground of the axial progression with the raised podium at its terminus.[13] Consequently, the reason a building can operate as a capacity to modify itself in order to accept a different performance is because the building is *typologically* suitable for the change. The reason a Roman basilica can operate as a Christian church of worship is because both buildings seek to embody authority and veneration. The survival of the circular building over thousands of years is another example. As Aldo van Eyck (1918–99) articulated succinctly, the uniqueness of the circular configuration comes from the fact that its rim embodies the duality between centrality of looking inward to find a communal center and the peripherality of looking outwards until one finds the distant horizon. The rim prioritizes neither the center, nor the horizon, but embodies their co-presence. This configuration is in a way the embodiment of a human ideal that keeps alive the dialectical tension between the two modes of life—the communal spatially embodied by the inward centrality and the public ready to break insularity of the former in search of different formats of the human relationship.

As we ruminate upon the significance of this notion of type from the perspective of sustainability, it is obvious that a building survives the test of time because it participates in the articulation of the human ideal and is thus typologically successful. Such a building must be apprehended not as a form, but as a capacity to accommodate different situations and programs. What makes a building sustainable beyond the lifespan of its author depends on to what degree the building participates in the articulation of human ideals. From the perspective of typology, a building is sustainable not merely because it recycles materials and spaces of an old building and is equipped with devices, such as photovoltaic panels and geothermal tubes. Its role as a capacity to accommodate different programs over time precisely because it is of a human ideal, such as the dialectical balance between the individual and the collective, enables the building to implement a qualitatively different sort of sustainability. This is the sustainability of human artifacts and ultimately the sustainability of humanity.

This work has explored the philosophical meaning of Watsuji's *fudo* and its architectural significance in reference to sustainability. Of course, there are weaknesses in Watsuji's thinking, weaknesses from which this work is not exempt, either. One particular example is the insularity of the communal in reference to the public, of which Watsuji did not develop a fully-articulated argument and criticism, probably on account of the political milieu of ultra-nationalism. His discussion of the nature of modernity in Japan, characterized by a disproportionate relationship between the hectic and tumultuous urbanity, on one hand, and, on the other, the peaceful selfless openness of the intimate domestic space, ends up reinforcing domestic interiority as the antidote to urban disorder. This antagonistic relationship, rather than reciprocity, between the public domain and the communal at the level of the family naturalizes the deficiency of the development of public spaces, as if the proliferation of one is the eclipse of the other. In this regard, the issue of how to transform the solidarity of 'we' as a way of articulating the public did not acquire much attention in Watsuji's thinking. The problem of how to overcome this dichotomy and mutual incompatibility goes unquestioned and remains a topic that Watsuji did not develop intensively in his environmental philosophy.

Despite its weaknesses, the importance of Watsuji's environmental philosophy is undeniable. His notion of *fudo* that illuminates the indivisible linkage between the natural and the inter-personal rectifies any perspective on sustainability that focuses exclusively on the greening of buildings. One is reminded of what Colin Rowe (1920–99) defined as "the crisis of the object"[14] entrenched in Le Corbusier's (1887–1965) urbanism. In the middle of the city was an unrealizable tension. Skyscrapers were masked by discrepantly exaggerated thick foliage of a forest, not just of a park. The emphasis on the crystal-like shiny prismatic object and the dream to realize a bucolic natural and undulating landscape formed an inherent point of conflict in Le Corbusier's vision. With the current tendency to green buildings, however, "the crisis of the object" seems to enter into another intensified phase in which buildings are wrapped up with greenery to the point where buildings disappear. The point is not at all to claim that the presence of the buildings must be reinstated. Rather, the thickened dominance of green imagery, or green primitivism, must make way to take in a balanced view of sustainability that joins the scientific concern of climatic amelioration and of saving energy, with a series of inquiries into the notion of climate itself, its relationship with human culture, and most importantly its inseparable connection with the inter-personal. Watsuji's philosophy offers quintessential clues to these inquiries. For my view, the two-way movement from the climatic to the inter-personal, and from the inter-personal back to the climatic, finds its most efficacious instance from what Watsuji characterized as the "selfless openness" of the Japanese architecture. If there were no collective orchestration of the partitions, openings and doors, there would be no natural ventilation. This collective human intervention is the very basis for cultural creations, not for the much condemned destructions of nature and its resources. When it comes to the highest dimension of the inter-personal, Watsuji's philosophy stages a dialectical space for the regional and the trans-regional and their mutuality. Sustainability at this moment is extended to embrace shared human ideals and their particular localized expressions, of which climatic idiosyncrasies are some of the primary factors. In the end, the scope of sustainability as apprehended in this manner must be stretched to acknowledge that it regards not only natural resources and devices but also, adopting Watsuji's expressions, "who we are," or humanity. For these reasons, Watsuji's philosophy of *fudo* is still distinctive and enlightening, despite being theorized more than three-quarters of a century ago.

Notes

1 Tetsuro Watsuji, *A Climate: A Philosophical Study*, trans. Geoffrey Bownas, Ministry of Education Printing Bureau, 1961, p. 16.
2 Ibid., p. 14.
3 Ibid., p. 135.
4 Ibid., pp. 4, 12–13.
5 Ibid., p. 4.
6 William LaFleur, "Buddhist emptiness in the ethics and aesthetics of Watsuji Tetsuro," *Religious Studies*, 14, 2 (June 1978), pp. 245, 247; Tetsuro Watsuji, *Rinrigaku*, vol. 1, Tokyo: Iwanami shoten, 1963, p. 107 (LaFleur's translation).
7 Tetsuro Watsuji, *A Climate: A Philosophical Study*, p. 200.

8 Ibid., pp. 18–118.
9 Nobuo Kioka, *Fudo no ronri: chiri tetsugaku eno michi*, Kyoto: Minerubashobo, 2011, pp. 312–20.
10 Tetsuro Watsuji, *A Climate: A Philosophical Study*, p. 6.
11 Ibid.
12 David Leatherbarrow, *The Roots of Architectural Invention: Site, Enclosure, Materials*, Cambridge; New York: Cambridge University Press, 1993, p. 75.
13 Ibid., p. 76.
14 Colin Rowe and Fred Koetter, *Collage City*, Cambridge, MA: MIT Press, 1978, pp. 50–60, 62.

INDEX

Taylor & Francis eBooks

Helping you to choose the right eBooks for your Library

Add Routledge titles to your library's digital collection today. Taylor and Francis ebooks contains over 50,000 titles in the Humanities, Social Sciences, Behavioural Sciences, Built Environment and Law.

Choose from a range of subject packages or create your own!

Benefits for you

>> Free MARC records
>> COUNTER-compliant usage statistics
>> Flexible purchase and pricing options
>> All titles DRM-free.

Benefits for your user

>> Off-site, anytime access via Athens or referring URL
>> Print or copy pages or chapters
>> Full content search
>> Bookmark, highlight and annotate text
>> Access to thousands of pages of quality research at the click of a button.

REQUEST YOUR FREE INSTITUTIONAL TRIAL TODAY

Free Trials Available
We offer free trials to qualifying academic, corporate and government customers.

eCollections – Choose from over 30 subject eCollections, including:

Archaeology	Language Learning
Architecture	Law
Asian Studies	Literature
Business & Management	Media & Communication
Classical Studies	Middle East Studies
Construction	Music
Creative & Media Arts	Philosophy
Criminology & Criminal Justice	Planning
Economics	Politics
Education	Psychology & Mental Health
Energy	Religion
Engineering	Security
English Language & Linguistics	Social Work
Environment & Sustainability	Sociology
Geography	Sport
Health Studies	Theatre & Performance
History	Tourism, Hospitality & Events

For more information, pricing enquiries or to order a free trial, please contact your local sales team:
www.tandfebooks.com/page/sales

Routledge
Taylor & Francis Group

The home of
Routledge books

www.tandfebooks.com